# gRPC Microservices in Go

HÜSEYIN BABAL

MANNING
SHELTER ISLAND

Manning Publications Co.
20 Baldwin Road
PO Box 761
Shelter Island, NY 11964

| | |
|---|---|
| Development editor: | Doug Rudder |
| Technical editor: | Bartosz Solowiej |
| Review editor: | Adriana Sabo |
| Production editor: | Deirdre S. Hiam |
| Copy editor: | Michele Mitchell |
| Proofreader: | Meredith Mix |
| Technical proofreader: | Peter Hampton |
| Typesetter: | Gordan Salinovic |
| Cover designer: | Marija Tudor |

ISBN 9781633439207
Printed in the United States of America

# Get the eBook FREE!

(PDF, ePub, Kindle, and liveBook all included)

We believe that once you buy a book from us, you should be able to read it in any format we have available. To get electronic versions of this book at no additional cost to you, purchase and then register this book at the Manning website.

Go to https://www.manning.com/freebook and follow the instructions to complete your pBook registration.

## That's it!
## Thanks from Manning!

# *brief contents*

# contents

# *preface*

I started as a software developer in 2007, and over the years, I've seen the evolution of web-based projects and the shift toward enterprise applications. In 2014, I was introduced to microservices and have advocated for this modern software architecture ever since.

In my journey with microservices, I've used various technologies to develop and deploy microservices to production environments. A tool that caught my attention was gRPC, which is a high-performance, open-source framework developed by Google and built on top of HTTP/2. I was fascinated by gPRC's potential regarding microservices communication. Its support for multiple languages, including Go, and its ease of building cloud-native applications made it an obvious choice for me.

However, I soon realized that there weren't enough resources to cover all the pieces of microservices to help developers like me get started. There were individual tutorials like the Hello World program and a couple about Protobuf, but no comprehensive guides existed that explained gRPC and Protobuf with production-grade examples. Over time, I worked through the processes and learned to use gRPC to build microservices that communicate effectively with each other. gRPC has never let me down.

That's why I decided to write this book. I wanted to provide a comprehensive resource to help developers get up to speed with the technology and put it into practice. In this book, I have drawn on my experience with microservices and gRPC to provide a complete guide to building microservices with both gRPC and Protobuf. We'll write the code in Go, a popular programming language for building cloud-native applications and microservices. Throughout the book, we'll use an e-commerce application, deployed on Kubernetes, as an example to guide you on your own journey into gRPC and microservices. We'll also cover advanced topics such as error handling, testing, and security, which are vital for building product-grade applications.

I wrote this book to make it easier for developers like me to get started with gRPC, and I hope you'll find it a valuable resource. Thank you for choosing *gRPC Microservices in Go*.

# *acknowledgments*

Writing a book is never easy, and writing *gRPC Microservices in Go* was no exception. I have spent countless hours working on this book both in various cafes and at home, and while traveling, to produce comprehensive content.

First and foremost, I want to thank my beautiful wife, Emel, who has supported me throughout this journey. She has always encouraged me to pursue my passion, even when I was exhausted and felt like giving up. Her unwavering support and understanding have been a constant source of inspiration for me.

Next, I want to extend my heartfelt gratitude to my editor, Doug Rudder, for his support during several months of work on this book. His feedback, suggestions, and edits have been invaluable, and I could not have completed this book without him. I also want to thank my technical editor, Bartosz Solowiej; his attention to detail and thoroughness helped me refine and polish the technical aspects of the book. My thanks to everyone else at Manning: my project editor, Deirdre Hiam; my copyeditor, Michelle Mitchell; and my proofreader, Meredith Mix.

I want to thank the reviewers who provided valuable feedback during the writing process. Your comments and suggestions helped me improve the book's content and make it more useful for readers. Thank you to Alain Couniot, Alceu Rodrigues de Freitas Junior, Alessandro Campeis, Andrea Monacchi, Ashish Kumar Pani, Borko Djurkovic, Cameron Singe, Dr. Keith L Mannock, Dylan Guedes, Fatih Akturk, Germano Rizzo, Gowtham Sadasivam, Horaci Macias, Jeelani Shaik, Christian B. Madsen, Joel Holmes, Jonathan Reeves, Karthikeyarajan Rajendran, Kelum Prabath Senanayake, Manzur Mukhitdinov, Marco Massenzio, Michael Haller, Mikael Dautrey, Muneeb

Shaikh, Neil Croll, Nolan To, George Onofrei, Peter Hampton, Rahul Modpur, Rich Yonts, Ryan Burrows, Ryan Huber, Satadru Roy, Stanley Anozie, Syed Basheeruddin Ahmed, Tim Homan, Vadim Turkov, and Walter Alexander Mata Lopez.

Finally, I want to express my sincere gratitude to the Go, gRPC, and Kubernetes communities. Your contributions, support, and enthusiasm have been a constant source of motivation and inspiration for me. I am honored to be part of such a vibrant and dynamic community.

Thank you all for your support and encouragement throughout this journey.

# *about this book*

*gRPC Microservices in Go* was written for anyone who wants to apply production-grade practices from gRPC, Go, and/or Kubernetes to microservice applications that run in live environment. It starts with microservices theory and cloud-native application development, then dives into the technical development of microservices in Kubernetes using Go and gRPC.

## Who should read this book

This book will help developers design and implement their microservices projects using Go and gRPC in the Kubernetes environment. There are some examples of Kubernetes deployment and gRPC usage online, but this book provides a step-by-step explanation of a gRPC microservice life cycle, from beginning to production. For this reason, this book will be a good reference for architects, chief technology officers, and engineering managers in applying microservice principles to development life cycles.

## How this book is organized: A road map

This book has three sections that cover nine chapters.

Part 1 contains theoretical information about microservices and gRPC:

- Chapter 1 briefly introduces gRPC microservices and provides an overview of the book.
- Chapter 2 discusses microservices, including their communication patterns, and explains how to use gRPC during development.

Part 2 provides step-by-step instructions for implementing gRPC microservices and deploying them to the Kubernetes environment:

- Chapter 3 provides information about installing gRPC and related tools (e.g., Protobuf) for project development.
- Chapter 4 explains hexagonal architecture and how to use it in microservices. It also explains how to structure a Go project with gRPC clients and servers to build a microservices project.
- Chapter 5 explains how gRPC client–server interaction can be used in microservice service-to-service communication.
- Chapter 6 describes how important resiliency is and how to apply resiliency patterns to gRPC service communications. The primary goals of this chapter are reader understanding of failover scenarios and of recovering from them.
- Chapter 7 explains how to write unit and integration tests for microservices. This is especially important for the microservices environment because many changing pieces must be maintained properly.
- Chapter 8 goes deep into some of the Kubernetes resources and shows how to use them to deploy gRPC microservices to the Kubernetes environment. This chapter also covers how to expose services to the public.

Part 3 covers gRPC microservice observability in the Kubernetes environment:

- Chapter 9 focuses on observability and demonstrates how to integrate observability tools into gRPC microservices for better visibility on the entire platform.

## About the code

This book contains many examples of source code both in numbered listings and in line with normal text. In both cases, source code is formatted in a `fixed-width font like this` to separate it from ordinary text. Sometimes code is also in bold to highlight code that has changed from previous steps in the chapter, such as when a new feature adds to an existing line of code.

In many cases, the original source code has been reformatted; we've added line breaks and reworked indentation to accommodate the available page space in the book. In rare cases, even this was not enough, and listings include line-continuation markers (➥). Additionally, comments in the source code have often been removed from the listings when the code is described in the text. Code annotations accompany many of the listings, highlighting important concepts.

You can get executable snippets of code from the liveBook (online) version of this book at https://livebook.manning.com/book/grpc-microservices-in-go. The complete code for the examples in the book is available for download from the Manning website at https://www.manning.com/books/grpc-microservices-in-go, and from GitHub at https://github.com/huseyinbabal/microservices.

### *liveBook discussion forum*

Purchase of *gRPC Microservices in Go* includes free access to liveBook, Manning's online reading platform. Using liveBook's exclusive discussion features, you can attach comments to the book globally or to specific sections or paragraphs. It's a snap to make notes for yourself, ask and answer technical questions, and receive help from the author and other users. To access the forum, go to https://livebook.manning.com/book/grpc-microservices-in-go/discussion. You can also learn more about Manning's forums and the rules of conduct at https://livebook.manning.com/discussion.

Manning's commitment to our readers is to provide a venue where a meaningful dialogue between individual readers and between readers and the author can take place. It is not a commitment to any specific amount of participation on the part of the author, whose contribution to the forum remains voluntary (and unpaid). We suggest you try asking the author some challenging questions lest his interest stray! The forum and the archives of previous discussions will be accessible from the publisher's website as long as the book is in print.

# *about the author*

HÜSEYIN BABAL has been a software developer since 2007. Since 2016, he has built cloud-native applications with Kubernetes in major cloud providers. He has also worked with enterprise companies to help them with their DevOps and microservice transition projects. You can find him giving presentations at global conferences or doing live coding sessions on his Twitch channel.

# *about the cover illustration*

The figure on the cover of *gRPC Microservices in Go* is "Bohemienne de Prague," or "Bohemian woman from Prague," taken from a collection by Jacques Grasset de Saint-Sauveur, published in 1797. Each illustration is finely drawn and colored by hand.

In those days, it was easy to identify where people lived and what their trade or station in life was just by their dress. Manning celebrates the inventiveness and initiative of the computer business with book covers based on the rich diversity of regional culture centuries ago, brought back to life by pictures from collections such as this one.

# gRPC and microservices architecture

There are three types of companies in software architecture: those that are content with their monolith applications, those that plan to switch to microservices, and those that already use microservices in production. Each company has its reasons for choosing a particular architecture, but using microservices comes with its own set of challenges. For instance, when you decide to break down a monolith application into services, you need to figure out how to manage communication between the services.

In part 1, we will first look at the big picture of an e-commerce application, and then delve into microservices architecture and its critical requirements, such as fault tolerance, security, continuous integration/continuous deployment (CI/CD), public access, and scaling, among others. Proper communication patterns between microservices are essential, and we will cover this topic as well.

We will also introduce gRPC and show how it fits into a microservices environment for service-to-service communication. You will become familiar with gRPC and see how it prioritizes security and performance to give you a seamless experience.

# Introduction to Go gRPC microservices

**This chapter covers**

- Introducing Go gRPC microservices
- Comparing gRPC with REST
- Understanding when to use gRPC
- Applying gRPC microservices to production-grade use cases

Good architecture design and proper technology selection help ensure a high-quality product by eliminating repetitive work and providing the best tool kit for software development and maintenance. While microservice architecture can be implemented in any language, Go is particularly suited for building high-performance cloud-native distributed applications such as microservices in Kubernetes on a large scale. Microservices with gRPC communication have already enabled many companies to implement their products with small services based on their business capabilities and have let those services communicate smoothly with each other and the public. With the help of Go, the distribution of those services becomes easier due to its fast compilation, ability to generate executable binaries,

3

and many other reasons, which we will see in detail with real-life examples in the upcoming chapters.

gRPC is an open source remote procedure call framework, initially developed by Google in 2015, that helps you to connect services with built-in support for load balancing, tracing, fault tolerance, and security. The main advantage of this framework comes from being able to generate server and client *stubs* (i.e., object on the client side that implements the same methods as the service) for multiple languages that can be used both in consumer projects to call remote service methods and in server projects to define business logic behind those service methods.

Microservice architecture is a form of service-oriented architecture that defines applications as loosely coupled, fine-grained services that can be implemented, deployed, and scaled independently. The main goal of this book is to provide production-grade best practices for gRPC microservices so that, by the end of this book, you will have the self-confidence to implement the entire system on your own.

## 1.1 Benefits of gRPC microservices

Within a typical monolithic application, calling different business activities, such as calling a payment service from a checkout service, means accessing a class method in a separate module, which is very easy. If you use microservices, such calls will be converted to network communication. These can be TCP, HTTP, or event queue calls to exchange data between services. Handling network calls is more challenging than calling another class method, which can be managed with a simple error-handling mechanism such as try-catch blocks. Even monoliths are easy to use at first, but you may need to decompose them for several reasons, including slow deployments and inefficient resource utilization that affect feature development and product maintenance. This does not mean monoliths are bad and microservices are good; microservices also bring challenges, which we will look at in detail in chapter 2. With the help of gRPC, most of the challenges in microservices, such as handling network failures and applying TLS (Transport Layer Security) to service communications (see chapter 6), can be eliminated. By using these built-in features in gRPC, you can improve both the reliability of the product and the productivity of an entire team.

### 1.1.1 Performance

gRPC provides better performance and security than other protocols, such as REST with JSON or XML communication, as it uses protocol buffers, and HTTP/2 over TLS is straightforward. Protocol buffers, also known as Protobuf, are language- and platform-neutral mechanisms for serializing structural data, which you will see in detail in chapter 3. This mechanism empowers gRPC to quickly serialize messages into small and compact messages on both the server and client sides. In the same way, HTTP/2 enables the performance with server-side push, multiplexing, and header compression, which we will see in more detail in chapter 5.

### 1.1.2 Code generation and interoperability

Let's say you have a checkout service and a payment service that allow a customer to check out a basket that then triggers a payment service call to pay for the products in the basket. To access the payment service, you need to have request and response models in some place, such as a shared library, to access them easily. Reusing a shared request and response model seems convenient in microservices but is not a good practice, especially if you are using different languages for each microservice. Duplicating models in a checkout service, typically by creating another data class to build request objects and deserialize response objects into, is a better choice. This is all about preventing an incorrect abstraction, as you may have already heard the statement, "A little duplication is far cheaper than wrong abstraction" (https://sandimetz.com/blog/2016/1/20/the-wrong-abstraction). There is an easier way: choose gRPC to define your messages and generate client stubs so that you can inject this dependency and use it directly in whatever language you prefer. We will dive deep into code generation in chapter 3.

gRPC tools and libraries are compatible with multiple platforms and languages, including Go, Java, Python, Ruby, Javascript, C#, and more. The Protobuf binary wire format, as it travels on a wire like in a network, and well-designed code generation for almost all platforms enable developers to build performance-critical applications while retaining cross-platform support. We will see the details of why Protobuf performs well in interservice communication in chapter 3.

gRPC is getting more popular (https://star-history.com/#grpc/grpc&Date) because you can quickly generate client stubs to provide an SDK of your services within different languages. You only need to decide what kind of business objects you need to have. Once you choose which fields you need for a checkout model, you can introduce respective request and response messages. Remember that those messages are just definitions in IDL (Interface Definition Language) and are independent of any language specification. After you define your message specifications, you can generate language-specific implementations so that any consumer can depend on that source. This also means that the development language on the server side can be different than the client side since server-side methods can be generated as stubs on the client side for specific languages supported by gRPC.

In addition to business objects, you can similarly define service methods and generate implementations. Those service functions can be called after you initialize the gRPC client on the consumer side; again, this client is generated out of the box.

### 1.1.3 Fault tolerance

Fault tolerance is a system's ability to continue operating despite system failures. An idempotent operation has no additional effect, even if called more than once. Idempotency is key to a successful fault-tolerant environment since you need to be sure that, once you retry an operation with the same parameters in case of failure or not having an expected state, it doesn't change the content of the actual resource. For example, we may want to retry a user delete operation in case of a network failure on response. If the operation returns the same result even if you call it more than once, we say this operation is *idempotent*.

If an operation is not a good fit for an idempotency use case, you must provide proper validation errors in a response message that help you know when to stop the retry operation. Once you guarantee this idempotency or proper validation, it is just a definition of the retry policy on the gRPC side. Fault tolerance also focuses on topics such as rate limiting, circuit breakers, and fault injection, which we will see in greater detail in chapter 6.

### 1.1.4   Security

In most systems, you may need a security layer to protect your product against unverified sources. gRPC encourages HTTP/2 over SSL/TLS to authenticate and encrypt data exchanged between the client and server. More specifically, you can easily set that authentication system up using SSL/TLS, ALTS (Application Layer Transport Security), or a token-based authentication system, which we will cover in more detail in chapter 6.

### 1.1.5   Streaming

Sometimes you may need to divide response data into several chunks in a paginated way that reduces bandwidth and returns them to the user quickly. Moreover, if users are only interested in specific pages, it is not meaningful to return all the data simultaneously. In gRPC, in addition to pagination, you can also stream this data to the consumer instead of forcing the user to do pagination to get the data iteratively. Streaming doesn't necessarily have to be on the server side; it can also be on the client side or both sides simultaneously, called *bidirectional streaming*. In a typical streaming use case, you open the connection once, and the data is streamed through this opened connection. You will see different kinds of streaming use cases in this book, particularly in chapter 5, when we implement a complete application.

## 1.2   *REST vs. RPC*

REST (Representational State Transfer) is a widely adopted protocol for microservices. Still, you may start to think about using gRPC if you have strict requirements such as low latency, multilanguage system support, and so forth. REST is based on HTTP 1.0 protocol that lets you exchange messages in a JSON or XML format between the client and server. On the other hand, gRPC is based on RPC (Remote Procedure Call) architecture that uses protocol buffers' binary format to exchange data over HTTP 2.0 protocol. This does not mean that REST is not compatible with HTTP 2.0; you can set up your REST services based on that protocol with a custom implementation so that it is a built-in feature in gRPC.

Since gRPC has built-in HTTP 2.0 support, you can also use unary and bidirectional streaming between clients and servers, resulting in high-speed communication. With REST services' default settings, multiple client–server communications can introduce a delay in overall system performance.

There are also cases in which REST is more beneficial than gRPC. For example, the REST protocol is supported in all kinds of browsers. Since gRPC support is minimal, you may need to use a proxy layer, such as gRPC Web (https://github.com/grpc/grpc-web), to easily communicate with the gRPC server.

gRPC has lots of advantages, such as being able to define messages to easily exchange data between services. Regarding readability, JSON and XML usage in REST have advantages, such as changing the request freely if there is no explicit business validation for the changed fields. In contrast, you need to follow some rules in gRPC to make a change. We will explain this in detail in chapter 5.

gRPC has a built-in client and server stub generation mechanism for which you need to use a framework in REST such as Swagger Codegen to generate client-side models. This becomes critical, especially once you have multiple services and maintain multiple SDKs for customers simultaneously. Now that we understand the differences between REST and gRPC, let's look at when it makes sense to use gRPC.

## 1.3 When to use gRPC

If you have strict requirements for browser support, then you need to think of using REST, because you will end up setting up another layer for conversion between HTTP/2 and HTTP/1. However, you can still use gRPC for interservice communication and attach a gRPC load balancer (http://mng.bz/BmZ8) to that service pool to expose API to the public for REST compatibility, which we will see in detail in chapter 9. Other alternatives include Twirp (https://github.com/twitchtv/twirp), an RPC framework built on Protobuf. Twirp lets you enable the REST layer for gRPC services in a way that allows you to access your endpoints, as in the following example, which sends a POST request with a JSON payload:

```
curl -X "POST" \
    - H "Content-Type: application/json" \
    -d '{"name": "dev-cluster"}' \
    ➥ http://localhost:8080/twirp/github.com/huseyinbabal/microservices-
    ➥ proto/cluster/Create
```

Polyglot development environments are ideal for gRPC integrations since using the Python client within the Checkout service to access the Payment service, which is written using Java, is very easy with client stub generation. You can apply the same strategy to your SDK generations for public consumers. Also, whenever you change your service definitions, the test fails on the client side, which is a suitable verification mechanism for your microservices.

You will learn how to test gRPC microservices in chapter 7. gRPC may not be the proper selection for simple applications such as startup projects that contain only one to two services since maintaining the proto files that contain service definitions is not easy, especially for inexperienced users.

It is, however, acceptable to use gRPC communication between internal services, but exposing a gRPC interface to customers may not be ideal, especially if there is no SDK for the client for gRPC service communication. If you prefer to expose gRPC without maintaining the SDKs for your consumers, then it is better to share your service definitions with them or provide a clear explanation about how to make gRPC calls to your gRPC services.

### 1.3.1 *Who is this book for?*

This book contains many explanations, code examples, and tips and tricks supported by real-life examples that can be useful for the following roles:

- *Developers who don't know Go or microservices*—They can take advantage of starting with introductory chapters about Go, microservices, and gRPC and learn production-grade techniques for gRPC Go microservices. Readers who already know microservice architecture can refresh their knowledge with the resources described in Go, which can be easily adapted to any other language.
- *Engineering managers*—They can improve team developer productivity by adding the best practices described in their playbooks. Applying techniques will introduce good visibility over the entire product that will help to quickly onboard new employees to the team.
- *Software architects*—There are many handy examples and architectural designs that can be potential references for their decisions for new products or features.

## 1.4 *Production-grade use cases*

As shown in figure 1.1, we will try to create an e-commerce product in this book with Go gRPC microservices that are automated within a proper CI/CD pipeline and live in a Kubernetes environment. In the following subsections, we'll visit critical parts of the diagram to see how important they are for a typical development life cycle, how gRPC makes those parts easier to handle, and which technologies to use and where.

There will be production-grade examples in this book in the following format:

- A completed project at the end of this book
- Code examples to better understand a specific topic and how it works
- Automation examples, especially with GitHub Actions to reduce repetitive operations
- Preparing artifacts for deployment
- Security best practices

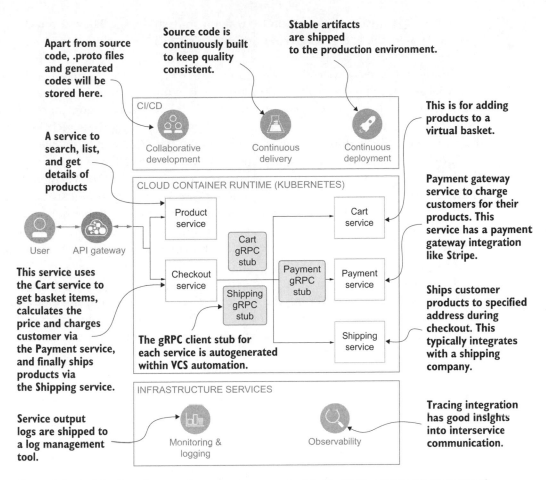

**Figure 1.1  Architecture diagram of an e-commerce product built with Go microservices on top of Kubernetes, including CI/CD flow and observability**

### 1.4.1  Microservices

Microservice projects are full of challenges, especially at the beginning of the project, and you will often hear the following questions in your architectural decision meetings:

- Let's implement microservices, but how micro should it be?
- Which strategy do we need to base our construct/decompose services on?

Dividing microservices by business capabilities is one of the options (http://mng .bz/rWnD), and we will use that distinction as we focus on real-life use cases and implement them in upcoming chapters. As shown in figure 1.1, we have five services to provide different business features, such as a Shipping service to ship products to the customer and a payment service to charge a customer's credit card using information in the checkout phase, which is composed of cart items. There are five business capabilities: product, cart, checkout, payment, and shipping. They connect using their generated stubs (e.g., Checkout uses Shipping gRPC stubs to call Shipping service functions).

Monolith-to-microservice decomposition will replace service function calls with network calls, which means you need to implement a fault-tolerant client for interservice communication. gRPC provides basic things like connection pooling and resource access so that service functions can be accessed using their gRPC stubs on the client side after adding autogenerated stubs to the Consumer service as a Go dependency. As seen in figure 1.1, the Checkout service can call the Cart service to get cart items, the Shipping service to get the customer's address, and the Payment service to charge the customer's credit card by adding respectively generated stubs of Shipping, Cart, and Payment services to the Checkout service as a Go dependency. We will look at dependency management in detail in chapter 5; you will learn how to work with dependencies and how to automate them to generate in a CI (continuous integration) pipeline.

Microservice architecture opens a gate to the polyglot development environment, which is very helpful for choosing the proper language for different use cases. It also allows the use of various technologies such as Neo4j for graph-related use cases, MySQL if there is a need for relational table structures, or Mongo for document-based data models. Microservice architecture also helps you to construct different small teams to assign code ownerships to a specific pool of services.

### 1.4.2    *Container runtime*

Managing an application environment may not be a real concern if you have a monolithic application because you can deploy this application into a set of virtual machines, and a typical load balancer handles traffic. Inadequate resource utilization, scaling problems, and risky deployments encourage people to move to microservice architecture. However, once you make the switch, because each service is independent, you need to start thinking of a distributed environment that needs proper management.

Kubernetes, an open source container orchestration platform, has already proved itself for application deployment management and many other production-grade use cases. The services shown in figure 1.1 will be all cloud-native applications and will have Kubernetes deployment specs defined for use within a CI/CD pipeline. Moreover, each service will run within a container and can be scaled horizontally based on the load.

gRPC needs a server address to dial in to call service functions. Kubernetes's discovery system is a good fit for finding the correct address because the server address is the service name of a microservice defined within a service spec. Suppose you have a proper naming convention for your services. In that case, you also have perfect integration between the consumer and service, with no help from service discovery products to see the actual address of a specific service.

Each service can have different behavior, such as resource requests, scale factors, language runtime, and so on. Again, they are just configurations within Kubernetes deployments that can be appropriately configured for each service. For example, say the Product service needs more capacity or scaling factors than other services since most customers search and view products during the day. You don't need to simultaneously scale all the services in Kubernetes like you do in a monolithic application. This can be handled by adding scaling factors and resource capacity to specific services.

The main output for each service will be a cloud-native application, which means you can deploy this service to any other container runtime, such as AWS Fargate, AWS ECS, even Docker for local development, and so on, with a little modification.

### 1.4.3 CI/CD pipeline

There are lots of operations that are candidates for automation within the microservices environment. Service artifact building, gRPC stub generation for specific languages, testing, code quality check, and deployment of services are some well-known examples. The more automation you have for this distributed system, the less stress you have during the development life cycle.

You can easily use gRPC tools to generate stubs on your local environment, but wouldn't it be better to generate them whenever some changes are pushed to the remote repository? You can also generate artifacts to deploy them to an experimental or stable environment after merging them into the main branch. Modern Version Control System (VCS) providers such as GitHub, GitLab, and Bitbucket already have that kind of integration, so there is not much custom implementation needed for this level of automation.

A green check after a CI/CD job execution does not mean everything is fine; there should be a way to check that the correct mechanism was used. Good coverage of unit tests; proper integration tests to check third-party integrations such as MySQL, Kubernetes, or AWS; contract testing for service-to-service communication; static code analysis; and vulnerability checks are a good start to have a reliable codebase in the main branch.

After a successful and reliable codebase, artifacts can be generated and tagged to be deployed to the user acceptance testing (UAT) environment and then the production environment for end users. Some best practices for deployment methodologies include a rolling upgrade, canary deployment, and blue-green deployment. The main goal with deployment is to ship the artifact, a Docker image in our case, to the Kubernetes environment and be prepared to roll back when needed. The decision to roll back the operation is not easy. Still, if you have a proper monitoring system, you can track error rates and user feedback to decide when to roll back or introduce a hotfix to the current version.

### 1.4.4 Monitoring and observability

*Monitoring* is a mechanism that allows teams to watch and understand the state of their systems, and *observability* is a mechanism that enables teams to debug their systems.

Observable systems are achieved mainly through metrics, logs, and tracing. Tracing context is critical to see any specific request's life cycle, which we will see in chapter 9 in detail. Let's say that a consumer uses an SDK to access an API via the API gateway. It propagates requests to four to five downstream services to handle all the operations and then returns to the customer. Having a successful response does not mean everything is good; it is not good if there is a latency within this life cycle. After latency detection, request flows can be analyzed by grouping by trace IDs that contain helpful information. Trace IDs in the requests and response headers can be injected quickly with a simple middleware that we will see in detail in chapter 9.

Monitoring is a crucial part of microservice architecture, because once you decompose a monolithic application into a microservice architecture, you must introduce a solution for better visibility. Service-level metrics, overall latency, and service-to-service call hierarchy are some solutions you may want to see in the monitoring dashboard. In addition to system-level metrics, the logs of the services are also necessary since they allow you to track application-level anomalies such as increasing error rates.

Dashboards, panels, and graphs for your system provide a good start for better observability. Still, we should focus on introducing new metrics and creating specific alarms based on these tools to notify you when you are away from your dashboards. As an example, Prometheus (https://prometheus.io), an open source event monitoring and alerting tool, can be used to collect system and application metrics, and there can be new alert configurations based on those metrics, such as "notify once the memory usage percentage > 80 for a specific service." Logs are also good sources of insight because you can calculate error rates in real time. You can even create alert configurations based on log patterns within modern log management tools such as Elastic Stack (Elasticsearch, Logstash, and other Elastic integration products).

A good monitoring setup can provide insights into both service-to-service communication and service-to-third-party integrations. For example, it will be possible to detect performance problems between a service and a database or a service to a third-party API that is out of the organization's control.

### 1.4.5   *Public access*

Public access is important for your product and for your business's reputation. For example, if a user can send unlimited requests to your product, this is a sign of bad architecture design for public access because products without a throttling system can cause resource exhaustion on the server side, negatively affecting performance.

API gateways are widely used to prevent these kinds of scenarios by following certain principles, such as quickly setting up a proper authentication/authorization system, introducing rate limiting to restrict users' request capacity, and so forth. If you already use Kubernetes, you can handle this with built-in features such as adding authorization and rate-limiting configuration to NGINX controllers; otherwise, you have other options, such as using API gateway products.

Resource naming is also crucial because it will affect the quality of product documentation. If proper naming is used for endpoints, it is easier to read the API documentation and consume those API endpoints smoothly. Optionally, you can implement SDKs for your product so that consumers can depend on that SDK feature instead of trying to construct requests, send them to API endpoints, and handle responses.

## Summary

- gRPC performs well in interservice communications because it uses binary serialization for the data and transfers it through the HTTP/2 protocol.
- gRPC allows you to engage in client streaming, server streaming, and bidirectional streaming, which gives you the ability to send multiple requests or receive multiple responses in parallel.
- Stable client–server interaction in gRPC microservices is easy because of automatic code generation.
- REST is popular primarily because of its broad browser support, but you can still use a gRPC web proxy (e.g., https://github.com/grpc/grpc-web) for REST-to-gRPC conversion.
- Due to its high portability, Go is one of the best languages for cloud-native applications, such as microservices in Kubernetes.
- Using HTTP/2 over SSL/TLS end-to-end encryption connections in gRPC eliminates most of the security concerns for a microservice.

# gRPC meets microservices

2

**This chapter covers**

- Comparing the advantages and disadvantages of microservice architecture to monolithic architecture
- Understanding communication patterns in microservice architecture
- Analyzing service discovery mechanisms
- How Go and gRPC boost reliable interservice communication and development productivity

The fundamental goal of any software development team is to implement a set of features in order to form a product and create direct or indirect business value. This product can be distributed as a package that can be installed on a computer offline or can be internet based and used online. Each programming language has its own packaging methodology; for example, you can use a WAR or JAR file for Java projects or a binary executable for Go projects. We call this *monolithic architecture*: one or more features/modules are packaged as one product that completes related tasks within a distributable object. When scalability problems arise, alternative solutions like microservice architecture are popular, as the application is decomposed into services based on their business capabilities. This decomposition enables the deployment of each service independently, which we will see in detail in chapter 8. Interservice communication stability is imperative to providing data consistency among services. This chapter will show how important gRPC is for interservice communication.

## 2.1 Monolithic architecture

In monolithic architecture, the different components of a monolithic application are combined into a single-tiered and unified software application that can contain a user interface, a server, and database modules that are all managed in one place. Monolithic architecture is especially helpful when developing the initial version of a product, as it helps you get familiar with business domains without having to tackle nonfunctional challenges. However, it is suggested that you assess your product periodically to understand whether it is the right time to move to microservice architecture. Now that we know what monolithic architecture looks like, let's look at its pros and cons.

### 2.1.1 Development

All modern IDEs are designed to support monolithic applications. For example, you can open a multimodule Maven project in IntelliJ IDEA (https://www.jetbrains.com/idea/) or create a modular Go project with GoLand (https://www.jetbrains.com/go/) that you can easily open and navigate within the codebase.

However, problems can arise as your codebase grows. For example, suppose you have many modules within a monolithic application, and you try to open them simultaneously. In that case, it is possible to overload the IDE, which negatively affects productivity; it also may not be necessary to open them all if you don't need some of them.

Additionally, if you do not have proper isolation for your test cases, you may run all the tests any time you make a small change in your codebase. The bigger the codebase, the longer the compile and testing time.

### 2.1.2 Deployment

Deploying a monolithic application means copying a standalone package or folder hierarchy to the server or a container runtime. However, monoliths may be an obstacle to frequent deployments in continuous deployment because they are hard to deploy and test in a reasonable time interval. You need to deploy the entire application, even if you introduce just a small change to a specific component. For example, say that we introduced a small change in the newsletter component responsible for serving the newsletter, and we want to test and deploy it to production. We would need to run all the tests, even though we haven't changed anything in other components, such as payment, order, and so on. In the same way, we need to build the system to generate one artifact, even though the changes are only in the newsletter component.

However, deploying a monolithic application might have more significant problems, especially if multiple teams share this application. Flaky tests and broken functionalities other teams introduce may interrupt the entire deployment, and you may want to revert it.

### 2.1.3   Scaling

Monolithic applications can be quickly scaled by putting them behind a load balancer, which enables client requests to be proxied to downstream monolithic applications in physical servers or to container runtimes. However, it may not make sense from a cost perspective because those applications are exact copies of each other, even if you don't need all the components to be scaled at the same priority level. Let's look at a simple example to better understand this utilization problem.

Let's say that you have a monolithic application that needs 16 GB of memory, and the most critical out of 10 modules is customer service. When you scale this monolithic application by 2, you will end up with 32 GB of memory allocation. Let's say that the custom module needs 2 GB of memory to run efficiently. Wouldn't it be better to scale just the customer module that needs an extra 2 GB of memory by 2 instead of 16 GB?

Distributing monolithic application modules to different teams for fast feature implementation is another challenging scaling problem. Once you decide to use monolithic architecture, you commit to the technology stack long term. Layers in monolithic applications are tightly coupled in-process calls developed with the same technology for interoperability. As a developer or architect, it would be harder to try another technology stack (once one became available). Let's look at the driving factors to scaling next.

## 2.2   Scale cube

Plenty of driving factors can force you to change your architecture, and scalability is one of them, for performance reasons. A *scale cube* is a three-dimensional scalability model of an application. Those dimensions are *X-axis scaling*, *Y-axis scaling*, and *Z-axis scaling*, as shown in figure 2.1.

### 2.2.1   X-axis scaling

X-axis scaling consists of running multiple copies of the same application behind a load balancer. In Kubernetes, load balancing is handled by Service resources (http://mng.bz/x4Me), which proxy requests to available backend instances that live in Pod resources (https://kubernetes.io/docs/concepts/workloads/pods/), which we will see in chapter 8 in detail. Those instances share the load, so if there are N copies, every instance can handle 1/N of the load. Some of the main drawbacks of this scaling model are that since each copied instance has access to all data, the instances need more memory than required and that there is no advantage to reducing the complexity of growing the codebase.

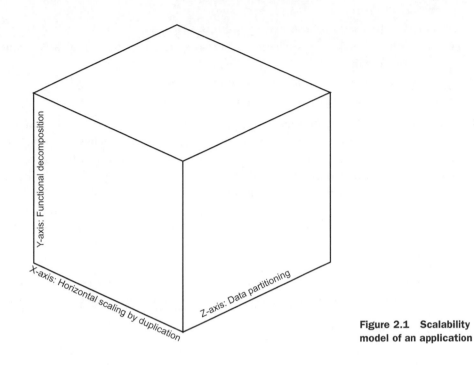

**Figure 2.1   Scalability
model of an application**

### 2.2.2   *Z-axis scaling*

Z-axis scaling is like X-axis scaling since the application is copied to instances. The main difference is that each application is responsible for just a subset of data, which results in cost savings. Since data is partitioned across services, it also improves fault tolerance, as only some data will be inaccessible to the user.

Building Z-axis scaling is challenging because it introduces extra complexity to the application. You also need to find an effective way to repartition data for data recovery.

### 2.2.3   *Y-axis scaling*

In Y-axis scaling, scaling means splitting the application by feature instead of having multiple copies. For example, you might decompose your application into a set of services with a couple of related functions. Now that we understand the pros and cons of monolithic architecture and scalability models, let's look at how microservices architecture is a form of Y-axis scaling.

## 2.3   *Microservice architecture*

Microservice architecture is an architectural style that defines an application as a collection of services. Those applications mainly have the following characteristics:

- They are loosely coupled, which allows you to create highly maintainable and testable services.
- Each of the services can be deployed and scaled independently.

- They are focused on business capabilities.
- Each service or set of services can be easily assigned to a dedicated team for code ownership.
- There is no need for long-term commitment to the technology stack.
- If one of the services fails, other services can continue to be used.

First, you must decide if microservice architecture is well suited for your product architecture. As said previously, starting with monolithic architecture is a best practice because it allows you to understand your business capabilities. Once you start having scalability problems, less productive development, or longer release life cycles, you can reassess your environment to see if functional decomposition is a good fit for your application. Once you decide to use microservice architecture, you might have independently scalable services, small projects that contain specific context during development only, and faster deployments due to faster test verification and small release artifacts.

Let's assume you are familiar with your business model and know how to decompose your application into small services. You will have other challenges not visible in monolithic applications, such as handling data consistency and interservice communication.

### 2.3.1   *Handling data consistency*

Having consistent data is essential for almost any kind of application. In monolithic architecture, data consistency is generally ensured by transactions. A *transaction* is a series of actions that should be completed successfully; all operations are automatically rolled back if even one action fails. To have consistent data, the transaction begins first, actual business logic is executed, and then the transaction is committed for a successful case or rolled back in case of failure. As an example, let's assume that once `Order :create()` method is executed, it calls a series of actions, such as `Payment:create()` and `Shipping:start()`. If both `Payment` and `Shipping` operations succeed, it will successfully commit `Order` status as `SUCCESS`. Likewise, if the `Shipping` operation fails, it rolls back the `Payment` operation and marks the `Order` operation as `FAILED` (see figure 2.2).

A typical transaction can be expressed with the steps *begin* and *commit/rollback*, during which you begin a transaction and execute the actual operation; then, you may end up committing data to the data store or rolling back the entire operation. Now that we understood that data consistency can be easily handled in monolithic architecture, let's look at how it is handled in microservice architecture.

### 2.3.2   *Saga pattern*

Transactions are a critical part of an application responsible for maintaining data consistency. In a monolithic application, there is a single data source in the same application, but once you switch to microservices architecture, the data state is spread across services. Each of the services has its own data store, which means a single transaction cannot handle the data's consistency. To have data consistency in a distributed system, you have two options: *two-phase commit* and saga. *2PC* (two-phase commit) coordinates all the processes that form distributed atomic transactions and determines whether

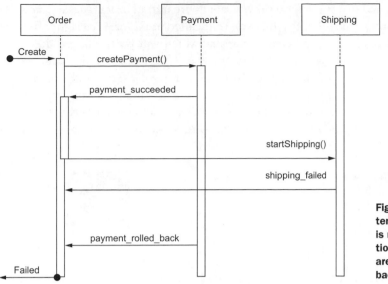

**Figure 2.2 The consistency of the `Order` data is managed by transaction boundaries, which are committed and rolled back.**

they should be committed or aborted. A *saga* is a sequence of local transactions that updates each service and publishes another message to trigger another local transaction on the next service.

Because transaction steps are spanned across the services, they cannot be handled with an annotation or two lines of code. However, there are widely used practices with saga, so you don't need to reinvent the wheel for your use cases. Choreography- and orchestrator-based sagas are the most popular patterns for interservice communication to have consistent data.

### 2.3.3 Choreography-based saga

A *choreography-based saga* is a pattern in which each service executes its local transaction and publishes an event to trigger the next service to execute its local transaction. Whenever a saga is created, it can be completed in the following patterns:

- Service returns the result to the client once the saga is completed. It receives an event to update its domain object's status as succeeded or failed.
- A saga is created, and the client starts to poll the next service to get either a succeeded or failed response. The unique identifier to start polling should be directly returned when the saga is created.
- A saga is created, and the client uses a WebSocket connection in which the service sends the result back using WebSocket protocol. A saga will be completed once the succeeded or failed result is returned.

Now let's look at how to apply one of these notations to a real-life use case for order creation flow.

In a typical order creation flow, a saga is created in Order Service, and Order is created with a PENDING state. It sends an event called order_created right after Order is persisted and consumed by Payment Service, which will try to charge the customer and send another event: payment_created or payment_failed. If it fails, Order Service will be notified, and Order will be marked as FAILED. Shipping Service will consume the event and initiate the shipping process if it is successful. Finally, it will create another event for failure or success, which will cause Order's status to be marked as FAILED or SUCCESS. A high-level diagram of communication with a choreography-based saga in shown in figure 2.3.

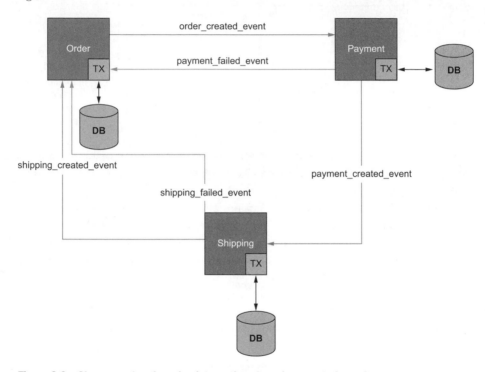

**Figure 2.3   Choreography of service interactions by using event channels**

Service communications over queue can be handled in two ways:

- *Command channels*—The publisher sends a message directly to the next service with a replyToChannel parameter so that it can notify the consumer once it completes the operation and commits the transaction. The main drawback of this pattern is that the publisher needs to know the location of the next service.
- *Pub/sub mechanism*—The publisher publishes a domain event, and interested consumers can consume messages to process and commit a local transaction. The main disadvantage of this notation is that it is a possible single point of failure since all the subscribers use one broker technology and all the events are sent to consumers.

Let's look at how we can use *command channel notation*: asynchronous communication that needs extra information in events to decide what to do next. In addition to the fields that form the actual data, a particular field, called a `replyTo` channel, is injected so that the consumer service can send the result back to that channel. It is also best practice to add some correlation ID to these events to see the whole picture of a specific series of events, as shown in figure 2.4.

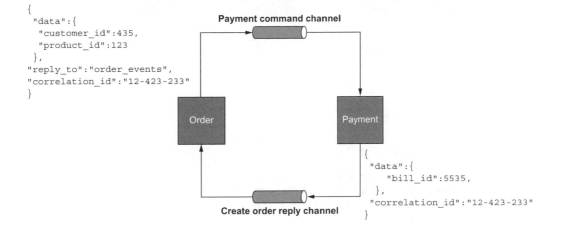

**Figure 2.4   The Order service sends an event to the payment command channel after the local transaction. The Payment service charges the customer and sends the ID of the bill, which was created after successful payment, back to the create order reply channel, which is already specified in the Order event.**

This type of communication is widely used in another microservice communication pattern called an orchestration-based saga. Let's look at this pattern to see how data consistency is guaranteed in a microservice architecture.

### 2.3.4   *Orchestrator-based saga*

Let's rework the Order service's creation flow to create an order saga using an orchestration-based saga pattern. An *orchestration-based saga* consists of an orchestrator and participants, and the orchestrator tells participants what to do. The orchestrator can communicate with participants using a command channel or request/response style. It connects participants individually to tell them to execute their local transactions and decides the next step based on this response.

Whenever you send a create order request to the Order service, it initiates a saga responsible for running a series of steps to complete the operations. When it calls the Payment service to charge the customer for that specific order, it can return a success or a failure. If it returns a success, the create order saga continues with the next step, shipping, in our case. If it fails in the Payment service, the saga runs a compensation transaction to undo the operation, which is a refund in this step. If the create order saga runs all the steps successfully, the order status will be saved as succeeded. Remember that if the saga fails at any specific step, it runs compensation transactions from the bottom up. For example, if it fails in shipping, it will execute `Payment:refund()` and `Order:cancel()`, such as a rollback operation for order creation, as seen in figure 2.5.

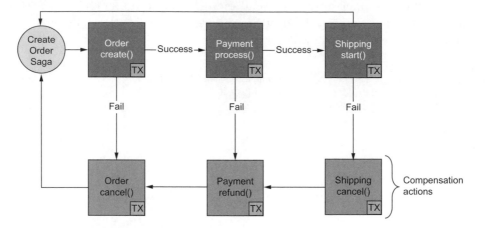

**Figure 2.5  An orchestrator for an order creation creates an order and payment process, and the Shipping service starts to complete the order flow. It runs a compensation transaction in case of failure, and this is executed from the bottom up.**

We will use the request/response style to complete a saga flow for interservice communication. Each service should know the address of all other services to connect. Let's take a closer look at how services find each other in microservice architecture.

## 2.4  *Service discovery*

Service discovery is the operation in which service locations are managed and exposed outside to let each service find the next one for step execution. There are two types of service discovery:

- *Client-side service discovery*—In this notation, a service discovery tool allows applications to report their locations during startup, as shown in figure 2.6. Client applications have direct connections to the service registry, and they query the location of a specific service by providing some criteria, like the service name, a unique identifier.
- *Server-side service discovery*—A load balancer integrates with the service registry to resolve downstream services. Client applications connect to services via the load balancer instead of using the service registry to resolve the exact location, as visualized in figure 2.7.

Apart from those two discovery mechanisms, container orchestration platforms such as Kubernetes have built-in service discovery mechanisms that allow you to access any service by its name, which we will see in detail in chapter 8. Now that we understand service discovery, which enables services to communicate with each other, let's see how gRPC comes into play.

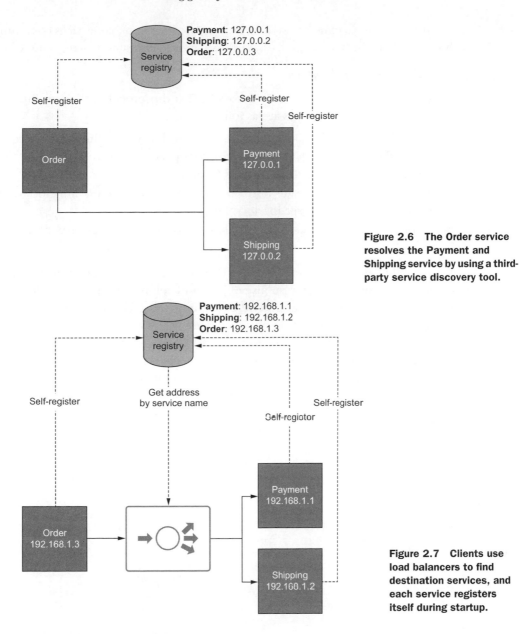

**Figure 2.6   The Order service resolves the Payment and Shipping service by using a third-party service discovery tool.**

**Figure 2.7   Clients use load balancers to find destination services, and each service registers itself during startup.**

## 2.5   *Using gRPC for interservice communication*

gRPC is a modern, lightweight communication protocol and a high-performance RPC framework introduced by Google. It can efficiently connect services in a microservices environment with built-in support for load balancing, tracing, health checking, and authentication. gRPC provides easy-to-use and efficient communication using protocol buffers, an open source mechanism for serializing structured data. Let's consider the minimum set of steps to use gRPC and protocol buffers to make services communicate with each other (i.e., exchange messages) using autogenerated Golang source code.

### 2.5.1  *Working with protocol buffers*

Let's revisit the order creation flow to use gRPC and protocol buffers for interservice communication. The ideal steps are as follows:

1  Define the proto files that contain message and service definitions. These can be inside the current project or in a separate repository independently maintained.
2  Generate the client and server stubs from the .proto file.
3  Implement the server-side business logic by using one of the supported languages (https://www.grpc.io/docs/languages/).
4  Implement the client-side business logic to connect services through the stub.
5  Run the service and client.

Any .proto file has message definitions and service functions in common. The message may refer to a request object, response object, and commonly used *enums* for a typical service in a microservices environment. For example, the Payment service would have a `CreatePaymentRequest` message to be consumed by the Order service. In the same way, `CreatePaymentResponse` can return `bill_id` to the Order service to store it as a separate field in the Order service's entity. Having just these messages is insufficient, so we need to define services to use those request and response messages. `Create` service functions can take `CreatePaymentRequest` as a function parameter and return `CreatePayment-Response` as a function return signature. These input and output parameters to service functions are important because they directly affect client-side usability:

```
message CreatePaymentRequest {
    int user_id = 1;
    float64 price = 2;
}

message CreatePaymentResponse {
    int bill_id = 1;
}

service Payment {
    RPC Create(CreatePaymentRequest)
    returns (CreatePaymentResponse) {}
}
```

`Payment` and `Shipping` stubs can be easily generated via a protocol buffer compiler for multiple languages so that any service, such as Order, can consume them, as shown in figure 2.8. For example, the Order service can call a `Create` function in the `Payment` stub, which uses gRPC protocol to access actual service endpoints in `Payment`. `protoc` is used to generate Go source codes from protocol buffer description files. In this case, `CreatePaymentRequest` and `CreatePaymentResponse` messages will be compiled into Go structs to be used in data exchange operations for marshalling/unmarshalling requests and responses (figure 2.8). Here, *marshalling* means converting a Golang struct into a byte array. You can see the internals here: http://mng.bz/AoVK.

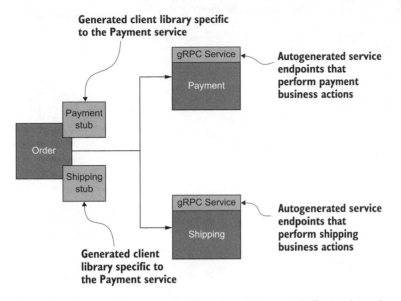

Figure 2.8   Interservice communication with autogenerated client stubs and server stubs

Now that we understand how to use protocol buffers to define service contracts (there will be more in-depth coverage in chapter 3), let's look at how to generate source code by using .proto files

### 2.5.2   Generating Go source code

**Using code listings**

GitHub Actions is used to simulate code listings in this book (repository: http://mng .bz/ZqpO). To run any code,

1. Go to the GitHub Actions of the repository you forked on your account. https://github.com/<your_username>/grpc-microservices-in-go/actions/work-flows/listing_execute.yaml.
2. Click Run Workflow and provide the listing number (e.g., 2.1).
3. You can see all the outputs of execution, especially the Run step that contains code listing output, if there is any.

A *protocol buffer compiler* (i.e., protoc), is a tool that generates a language-specific client and server-side implementation using a .proto file. We will see .proto file preparation in detail in chapter 3, but let's assume we have the following proto definition for the Payment service:

```
syntax = "proto3";      ⟵——— Protocol buffers version

option go_package="github.com/huseyinbabal/grpc-
➥ microservices-in-go/listing_2.1/payment";   ⟵┐
                                                 │  Package name of the
                                                 │  generated source code
message CreatePaymentRequest {
    float price = 1;
}

message CreatePaymentResponse {
    int64 bill_id = 1;
}

service Payment {
    RPC Create(CreatePaymentRequest)
        returns (CreatePaymentResponse) {}
}
```

You can use the following command to create client and server implementations of that .proto file.

> **Listing 2.1   Command to generate source code for Go**

```
protoc \
    --go_out=. \
    --go_opt=paths=source_relative \
    --go-grpc_out=. \
    --go-grpc_opt=paths=source_relative \
    payment.proto
```

This example is a simple request/response style called Unary RPC and will generate all the Go codes and put them in a location relative to input .proto files. gRPC also allows you to use streaming on both the client and server sides. To have a streaming response, you can modify your service functions in the .proto file:

```
service Payment {
    Create(CreatePaymentRequest)
    returns (stream CreatePaymentResponse){}
}
```

Streaming allows the server side to split data and return it, part by part, to the client side. The server returns a stream of CreatePaymentResponses in response to the client's request. Once the server sends all the messages, it also sends some metadata to the client to state that the streaming operation is finished on the server side. The client completes its operation after seeing this status.

Server-side streaming is beneficial if the server needs to return bulk data to the client. Streaming can also happen on the client side. For example, payment requests are sent to the server in streaming mode. The server does not need to send multiple messages, and it can return a single message that reports all the payment creation operation responses with their statuses:

```
service Payment {
    Create(stream CreatePaymentRequest)
    returns (CreatePaymentResponse){}
}
```

Streaming on both the client and server sides is called *bidirectional streaming*. It allows the client to send requests to the server continuously, and the server can return a result as a stream of objects. Since that operation is handled asynchronously, it is better to provide a unique identifier to mark which operation failed:

```
service Payment {
    Create(stream CreatePaymentRequest)
    returns (stream CreatePaymentResponse){}
}
```

Don't worry; we will examine this concept in detail in chapter 5.

### 2.5.3   *Connecting wires*

Client–server communication means service-to-service communication in a microservices environment. A service is a typical consumer that uses the client stub of another service. In our case, if you want to connect the Order service to the Payment service, complete the following steps:

1 Import the Payment service client stub into the Order service as a dependency.
2 Create a connection by dialing the Payment service from the Order service. Let's assume we already know the address of the Payment service since we use service discovery.
3 Create a Payment client using the connection object we created in step 3.
4 Call the `Create` method on the `PaymentService` client.

---

**Listing 2.2   Payment stub usage on client side**

```
var opts []grpc.DialOption

conn, err := grpc.Dial(*serverAddr, opts...)
if err != nil {
  // handle connection error
}
defer conn.Close()

payment := pb.NewPaymentClient(conn)
result, err := payment.Create(ctx, &CreatePaymentRequest{})
if err != nil {
    // handle Payment create error
}
```

In listing 2.2, we initialize a connection to address and pass this as an argument to `PaymentClient`. Notice that we use `defer conn.Close()` to be sure the connection is properly closed after the application closes. We don't care how the underlying communication is handled while connecting to two services. Everything is abstracted into a client instance, which is autogenerated by protoc into Go.

The protocol buffers compiler also generates a client implementation with a naming convention, `New<Service_Name>Client`, so that you can create a new reference for the client of a specific service (e.g., `NewPaymentClient`). When you call a client stub, it can return a success or failure. For resilient communication, it is better to retry failed requests based on some criteria. In the same way, it is better to provide a timeout to this execution to make an operation fail if the client cannot see the response within the requested time interval. These best practices are all about making data more consistent. If you have an order object in a pending state that lives there for hours, it is a sign of an incorrect communication pattern. As you can see in the last example, there is a `ctx` parameter, even though we did not explicitly define it in the .proto file. The Protobuf compiler just adds a context parameter to all the service functions to allow consumers to pass the reference of their context objects. For example, to cancel an execution if you do not get results in 10 seconds, you can use the following code:

```
ctx, cancel := context.WithTimeout(context.Background(),
10 * time.Second)
defer cancel()                              ◄———    Calls the cancel() method before
payment := pb.NewPaymentClient(conn)                exiting the current function
result, err := payment.Create(ctx, &CreatePaymentRequest{})   ◄——┐
if err != nil {                                                   Fails the execution
    // handle Payment create an error                             if there is no result
                                                                  within 10 seconds

}
```

## Summary

- Monolithic architecture is helpful, especially at the beginning of product implementation, but it is a best practice to switch to microservice architecture after you assess your product for scalability, development, and deployment problems, and then become familiar with your business capabilities and service contexts.

- Periodic assessment of your products helps you decide if switching to microservice architecture makes sense (functional decomposition according to the scale cube).

- Pub/sub or command channel mechanisms are examples of asynchronous communication, whereas the request/response style is an example of synchronous communication (e.g., gRPC).

- Choreography- and orchestrator-based saga patterns provide data consistency within a distributed environment.

- Protocol buffers help us define message and service functions to generate server and client stubs by using a protocol buffer compiler (i.e., protoc).

# Part 2

## Developing, testing, and deploying a gRPC microservice application

In part 2, we begin by showing you how to set up your environment to work with Go, gRPC, and related tools for your microservices application. You will also be guided through how to structure your project so that services are integrated smoothly. You will be introduced to hexagonal architecture, as well as a step-by-step demonstration on how to apply it to your microservices application.

Once you have structured your project, we'll move on to practical communication patterns using gRPC's built-in client-server interaction capabilities. Resilience is crucial for stable services, and you'll learn techniques to recover from failures during service-to-service communication. Hexagonal architecture uses layers, and we'll illustrate how to write unit and integration tests for each layer using Go.

After completing the application development, you will be introduced to Kubernetes basics and become familiar with its well-known resources. You will learn how to deploy each service to a Kubernetes environment using these resources. This includes proper security measures for publicly securing and exposing your application.

# Getting up and running with gRPC and Golang

**This chapter covers**

- Working with protocol buffers
- Generating stubs from .proto files
- Adding a stub generation process Into the CI/CD pipeline using Github Actions
- Maintaining .proto files in a scparate repository
- Maintaining backward and forward compatibility for protocol buffers

The communication between two services is just like two people talking: people use a telephone to connect, and gRPC does the same thing for interservice communication. In the same way that people use language to understand each other, two services use protocol buffers to exchange messages. It is crucial to select the proper communication style to create an effective relationship. Now that we understand that vital communication strategy, let's see how protocol buffers and gRPC are used together in microservice communication.

## 3.1    *Protocol buffers*

Protocol buffers allow you to serialize structured data to be transmitted over a wire. You can also define service functions and generate language-specific source code. The definitions of messages and service functions are written in a configuration file called a .proto file, which also contains version information for the protocol we will use (proto3) within this book. There are two other versions: proto1, which is deprecated, and proto2. The primary motivation behind the proto3 release is to simplify the syntax used in proto2. (For a detailed comparison of proto3 and proto2, see https://www .hackingnote.com/en/versus/proto2-vs-proto3.) You already saw a sample message in chapter 2, so let's dive a bit deeper this time.

### 3.1.1    *Defining message type*

Let's say you want to define a `CreateOrderRequest` message format in that each `CreateOrderRequest` has a `user_id`, `items`, and `amount`. In this case, the content of the .proto file would be like this:

```
syntax = "proto3"            ◁──────┐  Protocol version
message CreateOrderRequest {        │  Owner of this order
  int64 user_id = 1;         ◁──────┘
  repeated Item items = 2;   ◁──────  List of items for this order
  float amount = 3;          ◁──────┐
}                                   │  Total amount of this order that should be paid
```

Let's focus on the meaning of each part for each field in `CreateOrderRequest`.

#### FIELD RULES

Message fields can be one of the following:

- *Singular*—A structured message can have at most one of these fields. This field is the default field rule.
- *Repeated*—Any field with this rule may contain multiple values, including zero. The order of these items is preserved. In the previous example, multiple item values can be in the message (e.g., a customer ordered multiple products simultaneously).

#### FIELD TYPES

Field types are the data type of each field and can be one of the scalar types, such as string and integer. (See a complete list of the scalar types at http://mng.bz/N2VN.) These can be enums or any other embedded message type. The embedded type is `Item` in the previous example since it should also be defined in the .proto file as a custom type.

#### FIELD NAMES

The Protobuf compiler requires naming conventions for field naming since it generates source code for multiple languages by relying on those rules. The field name should be lowercase; if it contains more than one word, it should be separated by an underscore (e.g., `user_id`).

#### FIELD NUMBERS

Each field has a unique identifier in the message to identify the field in the binary message format. Since field numbers are unique identifiers for the fields, those numbers shouldn't be changed to provide a backward compatibility guarantee. If you want to remove a field, it is best to reserve it with the `reserved` keyword before removing it to prevent future definitions with the same field number or name. You can also reserve those fields by using their field numbers one by one or by a range with the help of the `to` keyword. For example, removing the `customer_id` field with field number 3 and adding a new field with the same field name or number with a different type will cause problems. If the client has the old message definition and the server has the new one, a data compatibility problem will result because they contain the same field but the data types are different:

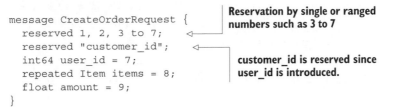

```
message CreateOrderRequest {
  reserved 1, 2, 3 to 7;          ◁──     Reservation by single or ranged
                                          numbers such as 3 to 7
  reserved "customer_id";         ◁──
  int64 user_id = 7;                      customer_id is reserved since
  repeated Item items = 8;                user_id is introduced.
  float amount = 9;
}
```

Required fields in a message can be thought of as frequently used fields since you cannot skip them as you can for optional fields. It is a best practice to reserve some numbers between 1 and 15 for the fields that can be frequently used since the numbers take 1 byte to encode in that range. For example, if you introduce a field with the name `correlation_id`, and it is used in almost all types of requests, you can assign one of the pre-reserved numbers for this new field. In the same way, it takes 2 bytes to encode numbers from 16 to 2,047. Giving frequently used fields numbers between 1 and 15 will increase performance quality. Now that we understand how to create a simple message, let's look at how protocol buffer messages are converted into a binary wire format.

### 3.1.2   Protocol buffer encoding

The main goal of protocol buffer encoding is to convert .proto file content into a binary format to send over a wire. The protocol buffer compiler uses a set of rules to convert messages to a binary format for better performance during marshalling (serializing), sending (over a wire), and unmarshalling (deserializing) this data. Let's analyze the example that follows and see how protocol buffer encoding works under the hood.

The `CreateOrderRequest` message has only one field, `user_id`, with type `int`, and field number 1. We compiled this message and used it in our production code:

```
// order.proto
message CreateOrderRequest {
    int64 user_id = 1;
}
```

```
// main.go
request := CreateOrderRequest{
    UserId: 65
}

// send a request via gRPC
```

The request object is marshalled by the protocol buffer (http://mng.bz/D49n) into []byte to be able to be sent over gRPC. Marshalling results in some bytes containing encoding information of the metadata and the data itself (see figure 3.1):

1   The metadata section is expressed with 1 byte and has the first three bits for denoting the wire type: 000, which is type 0 (Varint) since our data type is int. (You can see the whole list here: http://mng.bz/QPV6.)
2   The first bit of the data section is called the *most significant bit* (MSB), and its value is 0 when there is no additional byte. Its value becomes 1 if more bytes come to encode the remaining data.
3   The remaining bits of the metadata section contain the field value.
4   The data section contains the MSB (i.e., a continuation bit) to state whether there are more bytes.
5   The remaining seven bits are used for the data itself.

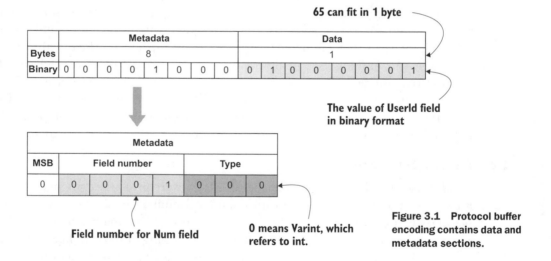

Figure 3.1   Protocol buffer encoding contains data and metadata sections.

A field's value can be anything based on your needs, and thus cannot affect performance. However, we can affect performance by following some rules for field numbers. For example, you can use numbers less than or equal to 15 for field numbers since that is the maximum number a metadata block can store. More metadata blocks are needed to express a specified field number. In the same way, if you want to store a data value greater than 127 (the maximum capacity of a data block), you need more bytes to fit that value in those data blocks.

Now that we understand how protocol buffer encoding works for a simple object with a field number less than or equal to 15 and for data values greater than 127 bytes, let's see how to encode an object with a value greater than 127. Let's say that the `CreatePaymentRequest` message has only one field, `user_id`, with type `int`, and field number 2. We compiled this message and used it in our production code:

```
// order.proto
message CreatePaymentRequest {
    int64 user_id = 2;
}


// main.go
request := CreatePaymentRequest {
    UserId: 21567
}

// send a request via gRPC
```

The Protobuf compiler will marshal the request object into a `[]byte`, and the metadata section will be encoded, just like the previous example and as visualized in figure 3.2. The data section will be handled this way:

1 Convert the decimal value `21567` to a binary value: `101010000111111`.
2 Split the binary value into seven-bit blocks: `0000001-0101000-0111111`.
3 The seven-bit block is for data, and the last bit will be used to store MSB.
4 Reverse the order of data parts (https://betterexplained.com/articles/ understanding-big-and little endian-byte-order/), which will result in `0111111- 0101000-0000001`.
5 Since there are three data parts here, the first will have the MSB as 1, the second as 1, and the 3rd as 0 since no more bytes come after that.

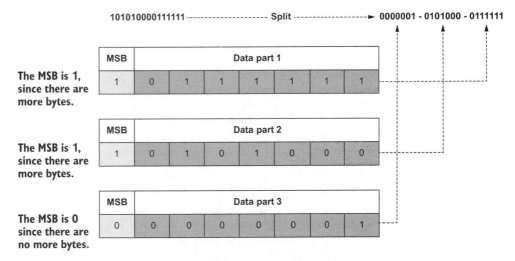

Figure 3.2  Protocol buffer encoding for the integer field values larger than 127

These examples can be expanded, but they are enough to better understand how protocol buffer encoding contributes to gRPC's performance for exchanging messages. In other words, instead of exchanging messages as they are, which will result in larger data size, they are converted into a binary format with proper encoding to reduce data size.

## 3.2 Generating stubs

gRPC Stub is a module that acts as an interface for the gRPC client. You can do several things using those stubs, such as connect and exchange data via streaming or non-streaming notation. The protocol buffer compiler generates the source code for a specified language, and that source code contains all the stubs. You can import generated source code into both the client and server sides to implement the business logic by following the contracts defined in the interfaces.

### 3.2.1 Protocol buffer compiler installation

To generate source code from .proto files, first install protoc, the protocol buffer compiler (https://grpc.io/docs/protoc-installation/). Then install two more modules to help protoc generate source code specific to the Go language:

```
go install google.golang.org/protobuf/cmd/protoc-gen-go@latest
```

```
go install google.golang.org/grpc/cmd/protoc-gen-go-grpc@latest
```

### 3.2.2 Using the protocol buffer compiler

Let's say you are about to implement a client-server application in which the client sends a create order request, and the server handles it. To do this, you can use the following .proto file to generate stubs using protoc:

```
syntax = "proto3";
option go_package=" GitHub/huseyinbabal/microservices/order";    ◁─┐ Package
                                                                    │ name for the
message CreateOrderRequest {                                        │ generated file
    int64 user_id = 1;
    repeated Item items = 2;
    float total_price = 3;
}

message Item {
    string name = 1;
}

message CreateOrderResponse {
    int order_id = 1;
}

service Order {
    rpc Create(CreateOrderRequest)
    returns (CreateOrderResponse){}
}
```

protoc mainly accepts the following parameters to generate language-specific source code:

- -I—To specify the import path where imported packages in .proto files are searched
- --go_ou—To specify where to put generated Go code for messages
- --go_opt—To configure options for Go source code generation, such as paths=source_relative, to keep the same folder structure after source code generation
- --go-grpc_out—To define the destination folder of gRPC-specific Go source code, such as calling a service function
- --go-grpc_opt—To configure options for gRPC-related operations, such as paths=source_relative, to have the same folder structure after source code generation

Let's say that the .proto file is proto/order.proto. In this case, the commands that follow will generate two files, order.pb.go, for message-related operations, and order_grpc.pb.go, which contains gRPC-related functionalities.

Listing 3.1  Generation Go source code

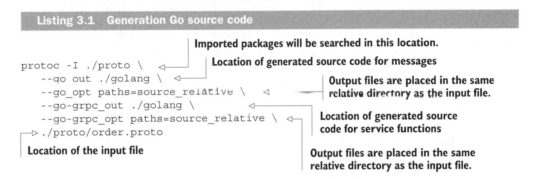

When you open the generated order_grpc.pb.go file, you see a function, `NewOrderClient(…)`, that returns an interface, `OrderClient`. There is a convention for functions like `New<ServiceName>Client` and `<ServiceName>Client` for the interface when `<ServiceName>` is the name of the service specified in the .proto file, which is `Order`. You can use the generated source code if the files are in your main project. Typical usage involves creating `OrderClient` and calling the `Create` method:

```
// Inside another module in the same project
import "GitHub/huseyinbabal/microservices/order"
…
client := order.NewOrderClient(...)
client.Create(ctx, &CreateOrderRequest{
    UserId: 123
})
```

Don't worry about the missing part for now. We will see complete examples in upcoming chapters. This example shows how quickly you can create a client instance and call methods specific to the order domain. You don't need to deal with connection-related operations; serializing/deserializing is handled out of the box.

Using autogenerated source code in the same project structure is easy, but what if you need to use those files as a dependency in external projects? For example, you generated stubs for the Payment, Order, and Shipping service and now want to use them in another project that can be written in another language other than Go. In this case, it would be better to maintain .proto files in a separate repository. However, keeping .proto files and their generations in the same location is easier if you are using a mono repo. Let's look at how we can maintain .proto files and generate them in a separate repository.

## 3.3    Maintaining .proto files

In this section we'll see how to prepare a separate repository to maintain .proto files, generate source code for multiple languages, and keep the files in dedicated folders. The primary reason to maintain .proto files in a separate repository is to be able to generate stubs for any language for use by any consumer. If we keep those operations within a microservice project that contains Go production codes, then any external non-Go consumer can depend on this Go project. Generated Java source codes in a Go microservices project may not be a good idea since they will never be used for interservice communication. They will, however, still be shipped and tagged with your production Go source code.

### 3.3.1    Proto project structure

Assume you created a repository, github.com/huseyinbabal/microservices-proto, with dedicated folders for each service to store .proto files. This project will have the following characteristics:

- .proto files are grouped by service folders such as order/order.proto in the root folder.
- There is a folder inside the root project for each language to store language-specific implementations.
- Generated source code for each service will be formatted as a typical Go module project since it will be added as a dependency on the consumer side.
  - As an example, the module name of the Order service will be github.com/huseyinbabal/microservices-proto/golang/order.
- Generated source code will be tagged: `golang/<service_name>/<version>` (e.g., `golang/order/v1.2.3`). This is the convention for the Go module to resolve the dependency that lives in subfolders in the remote repository:

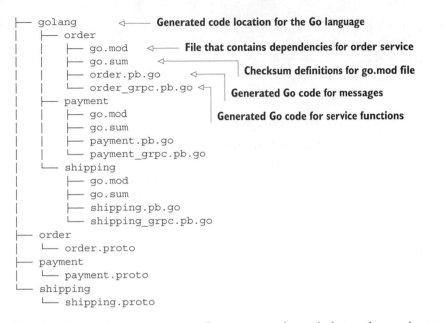

We already saw how to generate Go source code, so let's tag the project to make each generated service code downloadable as dependencies on the consumer side.

Golang's dependency version refers to a Git object as a tag, branch, or commit hash. In the dependent project, titles take a snapshot of the codebase to specify a specific release so that you can check any release for its release notes and use that tag. If there is no tag, the feature development is not read, and you can point your dependency to a branch or commit hash. Let's say you finalized your implementations for order, payment, and shipping services and want to use them for interservice communication or with external consumers. Tagging will make the repository discoverable for that version, a specific pointer to subfolders. For example, if you tag the repository github.com/huseyinbabal/microservices-proto as golang/order/v1.2.3, the source codes under golang/order will be available to the client. Tags can be different for each project:

```
git tag -a golang/order/v1.2.3 -m "golang/order/v1.2.3"
git tag -a golang/payment/v1.2.8 -m "golang/payment/v1.2.8"
git tag -a golang/shipping/v1.2.6 -m "golang/shipping/v1.2.6"
git push --tags
```

Once the tags are successfully pushed to remote, you can download the latest version or a specific version of the packages to use on the client side. You can use the latest version if you want to stay up to date on a dependency. You may also want to use a static version to be safe, since the latest tag can have incompatible changes that break the client:

```
go get -u github.com/huseyinbabal/microservices-proto/golang/order@latest
go get -u github.com/huseyinbabal/microservices-proto/golang/order@v1.2.3
```

This is just a brief introduction to module versioning. We will revisit this topic in chapter 5 in detail.

Manually handling these generations and tagging processes can be a bit painful as the service count increases. Next, let's look at how we can automate this process using GitHub Actions as an example of CI/CD.

### 3.3.2 *Automation for source code generation*

GitHub Actions is a CI/CD platform that allows you to automate a building, testing, and deployment pipeline. All the pipeline steps can be defined in the workflow file that GitHub can detect under your repository's .github/workflows folder. You don't need to be an expert on GitHub Actions to fully understand the examples, but, since we are using GitHub Actions examples to explain CI/CD parts of this book, you may want to look at the very short GitHub Actions Quickstart tutorial on Github: https://docs.github.com/en/actions/quickstart.

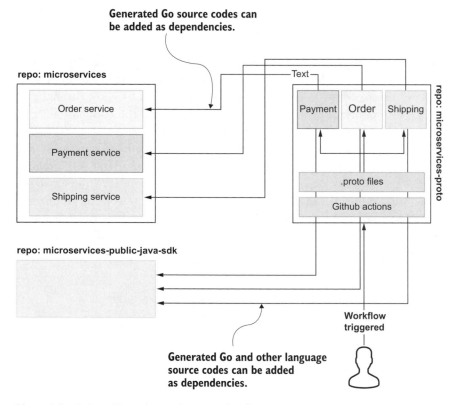

**Figure 3.3   Automatic source code generation flow**

As you can see in figure 3.3, Go source codes for Payment, Order, and Shipping services are generated using GitHub Actions whenever the user sends a change to the repository that contains .proto files for each service. The basic steps for the automation of .proto file compilation and Git tagging are as follows:

1  The workflow file is created under the .github/workflows folder, and the run.sh source code generator is in the root folder.

2  Local changes are pushed to remote and tagged by a specific version, such as v1.2.3.

3  Pushing tags triggers a workflow job execution.

4  Job execution installs required tools such as protoc and executes required commands for Go source code generation.

5  Step 4 is performed for each service with a matrix strategy (http://mng.bz/Pz58).

6  The Go mod init github.com/huseyinbabal/microservices-proto/golang/<service_name> command is executed for each service.

7  All the changes are pushed to remote.

8  New tags are created and pushed to remote by using current content, and new tags look like the code that follows.

**Listing 3.2   Go source code autogeneration**

```
#!/bin/bash
SERVICE_NAME=$1
RELEASE_VERSION=$2

sudo apt-get install -y protobuf-compiler golang-goprotobuf-dev   ⟵   Installation of required compilation tools
go install google.golang.org/protobuf/cmd/protoc-gen-go@latest
go install google.golang.org/grpc/cmd/protoc-gen-go-grpc@latest   Go source code generation
protoc --go_out=./golang --go_opt=paths=source_relative \   ⟵
  --go-grpc_out=./golang --go-grpc_opt=paths=source_relative \
  ./${SERVICE_NAME}/*.proto
cd golang/${SERVICE_NAME}     Initializes Go module
go mod init \     ⟵
  github.com/huseyinbabal/microservices-proto/golang/${SERVICE_NAME} ||true
go mod tidy     ⟵     Refreshes dependencies
cd ../../
git config --global user.email "huseyinbabal88@gmail.com"
git config --global user.name "Huseyin BABAL"
git add . && git commit -am "proto update" || true
git tag -fa golang/${SERVICE_NAME}/${RELEASE_VERSION} \
  -m "golang/${SERVICE_NAME}/${RELEASE_VERSION}"
git push origin refs/tags/golang/${SERVICE_NAME}/${RELEASE_VERSION}
```

You can see that the code in listing 3.2 is a standalone Bash script to generate the Go source code for just one service. This standalone script should be called for each service to generate the Go source code. In this script, we simply download the dependencies required to generate the source code from the .proto files. After the source code is generated, it is initialized as a Go mod project and pushed to a remote repository to be consumed by client-side applications. Let's see how this source code generation Bash script is used within the GitHub Actions workflow.

It is straightforward to run similar jobs in GitHub Actions using the matrix strategy, which allows you to use variables in job definitions to create multiple jobs with combinations of the variables. For example, you may want to execute a job for various services, or you can build numerous binaries by using different versions for one service. In the following example, source code generation is performed for order, payment, and shipping services whenever a tag is pushed to remote:

```
name: "Protocol Buffer Go Stubs Generation"
on:
  push:
    tags:                          Workflow is triggered once a
      - v**          <──────────   tag (e.g., v1.2.3) is pushed.
jobs:
  protoc:
    name: "Generate"
    runs-on: ubuntu-latest
    strategy:
      matrix:                                      List of services
        service: ["order", "payment", "shipping"]  <── to be generated
      steps:
        - name: Install Go
          uses: actions/setup-go@v2
          with:
            go-version: 1.17
        - uses: actions/checkout@v2                     Base version
        - name: Etract Release Version
          run: echo "RELEASE_VERSION=${GITHUB_REF#refs/*/}" >> $GITHUB_ENV  <──
        - name: "Generate for Golang"
          shell: bash
          run: |                         Go source code generation
                                              for each service
          chmod +x "${GITHUB_WORKSPACE}/run.sh"
            ./run.sh ${{ matrix.service }} ${{ env.RELEASE_VERSION }}  <──
```

Makes Bash script executable (pointing to the chmod line)

This example references protoc usage inside a GitHub Actions workflow (http://mng.bz/d16N), but you can still see the complete example in listing 3.2. (Refer to chapter 2, section 2.5.2.)

If this is the first time you've see GitHub Actions, workflow definitions may seem complicated, but don't worry; there are examples in other chapters for automating operations such as deployment. This automation can significantly increase productivity because all you need to do is add is the experimental messages and service functions, tag them, and let GitHub Actions complete the remaining tasks. (Refer to figure 3.3 for more precise insight into the automation described.) Now that we know how to compile .proto files and automate this process at a high level, let's look at what we can do to provide better compatibility between client and server.

## 3.4  Backward and forward compatibility

The software development process is not a one-time operation; it constantly evolves. This evolution always introduces changes to the system. If those changes do not affect existing users, it is called *backward compatible* change, which provides a graceful upgrade mechanism for your end users' integrations to your product. If a system is not backward compatible, it automatically forces users to upgrade their client library, which may not always be possible.

*Forward compatibility* involves processing input for the system with the latest version. A typical example is a web browser that can handle a newer version of HTML and simply ignore the part it cannot understand. Since writing software that is both backward and forward compatible is important, especially for client-facing APIs, let's examine some use cases you can use to validate whether the change is backward or forward compatible.

### 3.4.1  Adding new fields

As mentioned, gRPC lets us exchange messages between services, and those services should be carefully maintained, especially while changing something in message fields. Most of the time, you can add new fields to messages freely, but it is important to validate in advance if the new field you add is already reserved by field number or field name.

### 3.4.2  Upgrading the server but not the client

Let's say that `CreatePaymentRequest` has only the price field, and it returns `CreatePayment-Response` with `total_price`, which contains the final price, the sum of `price`, and VAT. In this scenario, the message is upgraded to v2 on the server side but is still v1 on the client side. The client side can live with v1, but the server side should change its implementation to support old client message types:

```
message CreatePaymentRequest {
    float64 price = 1;
}

message CreatePaymentResponse {
    float64 total_price = 1;
}

service Payment {
    rpc Create(CreatePaymentRequest) returns (CreatePaymentResponse){}
}


func (p *Payment) Create(ctx, req *pb.CreatePaymentRequest)
    (*pb.CreatePaymentResponse, error) {
    return &CreatePaymentResponse{
        TotalPrice: VAT + req.Price
    }, nil
}
```

Now let's add a `vat` field to `CreatePaymentRequest` and update the server-side implementation:

```
message CreatePaymentRequest {
    float64 price = 1;
    float64 vat = 2;
}

 func (p *Payment) Create(ctx, req *pb.CreatePaymentRequest)
     (*pb.CreatePaymentResponse, error) {
     return &CreatePaymentResponse{
         TotalPrice: req.Vat + req.Price
     }, nil
 }
```

Old clients will continue to send requests without the `vat` field, which will cause an inconsistency in the `TotalPrice` field. We can update the server-side implementation to use a default VAT if there is no `vat` in the request payload:

```
Func (p *Payment) Create(ctx, req *pb.CreatePaymentRequest)
    (*pb.CreatePaymentResponse, error) {
    vat := VAT
    if req.Vat > 0 {
        vat = req.Vat
    }
    return &CreatePaymentResponse{
        TotalPrice: vat + req.Price
    }, nil
}
```

### 3.4.3   Upgrading the client but not the server

If we upgrade the client but not the server, the client message type is upgraded to v2:

```
message CreatePaymentRequest {
    float64 price = 1;
    float64 vat = 2;
}
```

The server still uses the old message type, which does not expect a `vat` field, and a default value, VAT, for calculation. However, since the client sends this in the request, the server side will use the default value VAT and ignore the `vat` value within the request payload, but at least it will not throw an error.

### 3.4.4   Adding/removing oneof fields

Let's say you have multiple fields in a message that require one or the other but not both. For example, `CreatePaymentRequest` has both `credit_card` and `promo_code` fields, but you can send only one at a time. The `oneof` feature is used for enforcing this behavior instead of trying to put extra logic in actual implementation:

```
message CreatePaymentRequest {
    oneof payment_method  {
        CreditCard credit_card = 1;
        PromoCode promo_code = 2;
    }
}
```

After a while, remove the promo_code option from the list, tag the message type as v2, and upgrade the server side. If the client uses v1 and sends promo_code in the request, the information about promo_code will be lost on the server side since it is an unknown field. Removing a field from oneof is a backward-incompatible change, and adding a new field to oneof is a forward-incompatible change. If there is an incompatible change in your message field, you need to introduce an update to your semantic version (https://semver.org/) so that consumers will know there is a breaking change. Consumers will need to check the release notes page of the new release to make the necessary changes on the client side and avoid compatibility problems.

### 3.4.5 *Moving fields out of or into oneof fields*

This time a regular field is moved into or out of oneof group, which causes a data loss. Let's say that you have the following request to send CreatePaymentRequest:

```
message CreatePaymentRequest {
    oneof payment_method {
        CreditCard credit_card = 1;
    }
    PromoCode promo_code - 2;
}
```

After a while, we decide to move the promo_code field into one of the groups. The message is as follows:

```
message CreatePaymentRequest {
    oneof payment_method {
        CreditCard credit_card = 1;
        PromoCode promo_code = 2;
    }
}
```

If the client used the first message, set credit_card and promo_code fields, and sent them to the server with the second version of the message, then either promo_code or credit_card will be lost since you cannot send multiple fields for a oneof group.

Use cases about compatibility problems can be extended. Still, it is enough to understand that we should be cautious while changing fields, especially when reusing an already used field number or name. Changes should always be backward and forward compatible to prevent disruption on both the client and server side.

## *Summary*

- The protocol buffer compiler uses a special encoding operation to marshal data into a `[] byte` for excellent performance on the gRPC protocol.
- The protocol buffer compiler helps us generate language-specific source code that we can maintain in the same repo or an independent repository.
- GitHub Actions allows us to automate source code generation and tagging by using a workflow definition.
- Introducing changes that are always backward and forward compatible is crucial to prevent service disruption or data loss.

# Microservice project setup

**This chapter covers**

- Using hexagonal architecture for microservice projects
- Setting up tool kits for services
- Running a basic microservice application
- Making the initial request for running an application

It is very normal to ask, "How should I structure my project?" before writing the first line of your Go microservice project. The answer to this question might seem difficult initially, but it is easy to apply some common software architecture patterns that help solve challenges such as building modular projects to have testable components. Let's see how to apply those principles to a Go microservice project and perform some tests to see how gRPC endpoints work.

## 4.1 Hexagonal architecture

*Hexagonal architecture* (https://alistair.cockburn.us/hexagonal-architecture/), proposed by Alistair Cockburn in 2005, is an architectural pattern that aims to build loosely coupled application components that can be connected via ports and adapters. In this pattern, the consumer opens the application at a port via an adapter, and the output is sent through a port to an adapter. Therefore, hexagonal architecture is also known as a ports and adapters system. Using ports and adapters creates an abstraction layer that isolates the application's core from external dependencies. Now that we understand the general components of hexagonal architecture, let's dive deeper into each.

### 4.1.1   Application

An application is a technology-agnostic component that contains the business logic that orchestrates functionalities or use cases. A hexagon represents the application that receives write and read queries from the ports and sends them to external actors, such as database and third-party services, via ports. A hexagon visually represents multiple port/adapter combinations for an application and shows the difference between the left side (or driving side) and right side (or driven side).

### 4.1.2   Actors

*Actors* are designed to interact with humans, other applications, and any other software or hardware device. There are two types of actors: *driver* (or primary) and *driven* (or secondary).

Driver actors are responsible for triggering communication with the application to invoke a service on it. Command-line interfaces (CLIs), controllers, are good examples of driver actors since they take user input and send it to the application via a port.

Driven actors expect to see communication triggered by the application itself. For example, an application triggers a communication to save data into MySQL.

### 4.1.3   Ports

Ports are generally interfaces that contain information about interactions between an actor and an application. Driver ports have a set of actions, and actors should implement them. Driver ports contain a set of actions that the application provides and exposes to the public.

### 4.1.4   Adapters

Adapters deal primarily with transforming a request from an actor to an application, and vice versa. Data transformation helps the application understand the requests that come from actors. For example, a specific driver adapter can transform a technology-specific request into a call to an application service. In the same way, a driven adapter can convert a technology-agnostic request from the application into a technology-specific request on the driven port.

As you can see in figure 4.1, the application has a hexagon that contains business logic, and adapters can orchestrate the hexagon by using ports. CLI and web applications are two candidates for adapters; data is saved into MySQL or sent to another application.

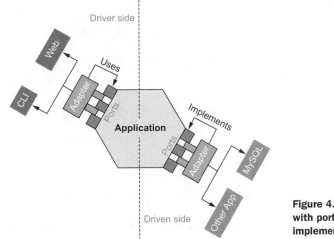

Figure 4.1   **Hexagonal architecture with ports allows external actors to use, implement, and orchestrate business logic.**

Using gRPC makes implementing hexagonal architecture easier because we become familiar with adapters out of the box by using gRPC stubs to access other services. gRPC can also be used to handle business models with the help of proto messages, which is especially helpful for duplicating models between hexagonal layers for better portability. Now that we understand the overall picture of the hexagonal architecture, let's look at how to start the implementation of a Go microservice.

## 4.2   *Order service implementation*

A clean architecture deserves a well-defined project structure. If we aim to use hexagonal architecture for microservices, having meaningful folder names that represent the isolation level is important. Let's look at the proper folder structure for a microservice project that uses hexagonal architecture for clear isolation between modules, as shown in figure 4.2.

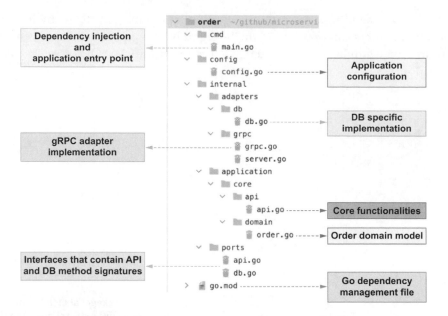

**Figure 4.2  Project folder structure of a Go microservice written with hexagonal architecture**

### 4.2.1  Project folders

While there are no written rules for a hexagonal architecture folder, the following folders are common in typical Go projects:

- *Application folder*—This folder contains microservice business logic, which is a combination of the domain model that refers to a business entity and an API that exposes core functionalities to other modules.

- *Port folder*—This folder contains contract information for integration between the core application and third parties. This can be a contract about accessing core application features or about specifying available features for a database system, if one is used for the persistence layer.

- *Adapter folder*—This folder contains concrete implementation for using contracts that are defined in ports. For example, gRPC can be an adapter with a concrete implementation that handles requests and uses an API port to access core functionalities, such as if you have an application with some functionalities and will expose it to customers. The functionalities can be CreateProduct, GetProduct, and so on, and you can expose them to the customer via REST, gRPC, and other adaptors, which will use the contracts of those functionalities, as defined in the port layer. We will revisit this topic and look at more advanced examples in later sections of this chapter.

Application, port, and adapter folders can be located inside an internal folder to separate operational functionalities, such as infra and deployment from application core logic. A cmd folder can also define an application's entry point, which also contains dependency injection mechanisms, such as preparing a database connection and passing it to the application layer. Finally, there can be utility folders, such as config, to provide a configuration structure so that consumers will know the possible parameters they can pass while running the application. Now that we understand what the folder structure looks like (see figure 4.2), let's look at how to implement the project step by step.

### 4.2.2 Initializing a Go project

A Go module helps you to create projects for better modularity and easy dependency management. Use the following code to create a microservice project called order and initialize it as a Go project:

```
mkdir -p microservices/order
cd microservices/order
go mod init GitHub.com/<username>/microservices/order    ⟵  <username> is your
                                                              Github username.
```

The `go mod init` command accepts a VCS URL to prepare the dependency structure. When you add this module as a dependency to another project, that project will resolve the available tag from the VCS you provided for module initialization. After the initialization, the go.mod file will be created, and initially it will contain only module information and the supported Go version:

```
module github.com/huseyinbabal/microservices/order    ⟵── Base URL of the module

go 1.17    ⟵── Supported Go version
```

As a final step for initialization, go to the order folder and create the following folders. Notice "-p" is used for creating parent folders that do not exist:

```
mkdir cmd
mkdir config
mkdir -p internal/adapters/db
mkdir -p internal/adapters/grpc
mkdir -p internal/application/core/api
mkdir -p internal/application/core/domain
mkdir -p internal/ports
```

### 4.2.3 Implementing the application core

Even though there was only one hexagonal layer in previous examples for simplicity, there may be multiple layers in most use cases. In hexagonal architecture, outer layers (outer hexagons) depend on inner layers (inner hexagons), which makes it easier to implement the application core first and then implement outer layers to depend on them. For example, the web or CLI layer depends on the application layer, as shown in figure 4.1. Since all the operations are performed on the `Order` domain object in the application layer, let's create the necessary Go file, add structs inside it, and add domain methods, once needed:

```
touch internal/application/domain/order.go
```

Domain objects in Go are primarily specified by structs that contain field type, field name, and serialization config via tags (https://pkg.go.dev/encoding/json#Marshal). For example, to specify a `CustomerID` field with an `int64` type of order and specify a field name as `customer_id` after JSON serialization (e.g., to save it in MongoDB), you can use the following code:

```
CustomerID int64          `json:"customer_id"`
```

`order.go` contains the following content:

```
package domain

import (
    "time"
)

type OrderItem struct {
    ProductCode string  `json:"product_code"`      ⊲──┐  Unique code of the product
    UnitPrice   float32 `json:"unit_price"`        ⊲──── Price of a single product
    Quantity    int32   `json:"quantity"`          ⊲──┐
}                                                      └ Count of the product

type Order struct {                                     ┌ Unique identifier of the order
    ID         int64       `json:"id"`            ⊲──┘
    CustomerID int64       `json:"customer_id"`   ⊲──── Owner of the order
    Status     string      `json:"status"`
    OrderItems []OrderItem `json:"order_items"`   ⊲──── List of items purchased in an order
    CreatedAt  int64       `json:"created_at"`    ⊲──┐
}                                                      └ Order creation time

func NewOrder(customerId int64, orderItems []OrderItem) Order {   ⊲──┐  Function
    return Order{                                                     │ to create
        CreatedAt:  time.Now().Unix(),                                │ default
        Status:     "Pending",                                        │ order
        CustomerID: customerId,
        OrderItems: orderItems,
    }
}
```

Status of the order ⟶ `Status     string      `json:"status"``

In this example, we simply implemented the `Order` data structure with an `OrderItem` relation and introduced a method called `NewOrder` to create an order. There is another package under the application, `api`, which contains another Go file to control the state of a specific order. During application initialization, we expect to see a dependency injection mechanism to inject a DB adapter (concrete implementation for a specific DB technology) into the application so that the API can store the state of a particular order in the database without needing to know the adaptor's internals. This is why the application depends on the interface `ports.DBPort` instead of the DB adapter's concrete implementation. The API interface uses this port to access the real DB adapter to save order information in the database with the `PlaceOrder` method:

```
touch internal/application/api/api.go
```

The content of `api.go` is as follows:

```
package api                                              Package for the order
                                                           domain object
import (
    "github.com/huseyinbabal/microservices/order/internal/application/core/
      domain"
    "github.com/huseyinbabal/microservices/order/internal/ports"
)
                                                    Ports for the DB adapter
type Application struct {
    db ports.DBPort        ◁──── The API depends on DBPort.
}

func NewApplication(db ports.DBPort) *Application {
    return &Application{
        db: db,        ◁──── DBPort is passed during
    }                        the app's initialization.
}

func (a Application) PlaceOrder(order domain.Order) (domain.Order, error) {
    err := a.db.Save(&order)   ◁──
    if err != nil {              Order is saved through the DB port.
        return domain.Order{}, err
    }
    return order, nil
}
```

The `Application` struct has a dependency in the DB layer, and you can see the `NewApplication` method that helps create an instance of the `Application`. Once you create an instance of the `Application`, you will see that each instance has a `PlaceOrder` method that uses DB dependency to save the order in the database. The original packages are used in the import statements, but you can use your package URL instead of github.com/huseyinbabal/microservices/order.... Now that we understand how the application core is structured, let's look at how to implement ports so that they can be used in the application and the adapters.

### 4.2.4   Implementing ports

Ports are just interfaces that contain general methods in each hexagonal layer. For example, we implemented the `PlaceOrder` method in the previous section, and if you look at it carefully, you can see that it implements the `PlaceOrder` method of the `APIPort` interface. The `PlaceOrder` method simply accepts and saves a domain object in the database. With this information, we can assume that whenever we want to create an application, we need to pass the DB adapter to it. The application saves an order in the database using the reference `db` via the receiver function.

Let's start implementing the API port with touch internal/ports/api.go, which contains an interface with just one method, `PlaceOrder`, as follows:

```
package ports

import
    "github.com/huseyinbabal/microservices/order/internal/application/core/d
    omain"

type APIPort interface {
    PlaceOrder(order domain.Order) (domain.Order, error)
}
```

While `APIPort` is used for core application functionalities, `DBPort` helps the application fulfill its functionalities. Let's create a DB port using the touch internal/ports/db.go file. `DBPort` is a very simple interface that contains the `Get` and `Save` methods, and, of course, it depends on the application domain model, which is `Order`:

```
package ports

import "github.com/huseyinbabal/microservices/order/internal/application/
➡ core/domain"

type DBPort interface {
    Get(id string) (domain.Order, error)  ⟵─┐   Gets Order by its unique ID
    Save(*domain.Order) error       ⟵──┐
}                                          Saves the Order domain into the database
```

The application depends on `DBPort` via the interface, but we need to pass a concrete implementation during initialization, so let's look at what concrete implementations of ports look like.

### 4.2.5  *Implementing adapters*

We must implement `Save` and `Get` methods to allow the application to save `Order` in the database. The ORM (Object Relational Mapping) library would be suitable for database-related operations in an effort to eliminate extra effort while constructing SQL queries. GORM is a very popular ORM library in the Go world, and we will use it for our project. Let's get GORM and MySQL driver dependency with the following command after you go to the root directory of order project:

```
go get -u gorm.io/gorm
go get -u gorm.io/driver/mysql
```

Now we are ready to create our DB file and add dependencies to your go.mod file. As you can see, GORM has an abstraction over DB drivers that you can easily use: touch internal/adapters/db/db.go. This file contains a struct for database models and related functions to manage their state. For the Order service, we have two simple models, `Order` and `OrderItem`, in which the `Order` model has a one-to-many relationship with `OrderItem`, as you can see in figure 4.3.

One of the best things about an ORM library is the ability to define these relationships with simple conventions, such as referencing a field in one model and applying

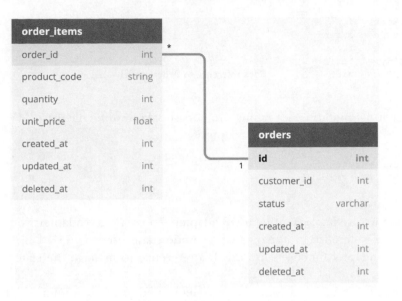

**Figure 4.3  One-to-many relationship between `orders` and `order_items` table**

it to another. A typical example of the `Order` model is that its field `OrderItem` refers to another struct. To set up a proper relation, there should be a reference ID on the second struct, `OrderId`, in our case. Finally, you can embed GORM to mark a struct as a domain entity, `.Model`, into the struct. This augments your domain model with built-in fields, such as `ID`, `CreatedAt`, `UpdatedAt`, and `DeletedAt`. GORM detects this relationship, creates tables in the proper order, and connects them. As you can see, the field names in figure 4.3 are in snake case. This serialization strategy is applied to the table structure before it is applied to the database, with the help of struct tags. Then we are free to add necessary packages and structs to the db.go file:

```
package db

import (
    "fmt"
    "github.com/huseyinbabal/microservices/order/internal/application/core/
    ➥ domain"
    "gorm.io/driver/mysql"
    "gorm.io/gorm"
)

type Order struct {            Adds entity metadata
    gorm.Model        ⟵──┘    such as ID to struct
    CustomerID int64
    Status     string
    OrderItems []OrderItem    ⟵──── Reference to OrderItem
}

type OrderItem struct {
```

```
    gorm.Model
    ProductCode  string
    UnitPrice    float32
    Quantity     int32
    OrderID      uint      ⬅——— Back reference to Order model
}
```

Having struct definitions is not enough to persist data into the database. We need to add gorm.DB as a dependency to our adapter:

```
type Adapter struct {
    db *gorm.DB
}
```

Let's assume we are implementing a DB adapter. To create the adapter, you need to pass a gorm.DB reference to it. Now that we understand how to add a DB reference, let's see how adapter functions use this DB reference to manage the state of order models.

The data source URL is a common parameter used to create a reference for database connections. We can create a connection to a provided data source URL by using a DB driver, which, in our case, is a MySQL driver, aliased by gorm/mysql. Error handling is also important here so that we understand whether the connection is successful and so that we can decide whether we should continue the initialization of the application. The following function is a good candidate for opening a connection to the database:

```
func NewAdapter(dataSourceUrl string) (*Adapter, error) {
    db, openErr := gorm.Open(mysql.Open(dataSourceUrl), &gorm.Config{})
    if openErr != nil {
        return nil, fmt.Errorf("db connection error: %v", openErr)
    }
                                                          Be sure the tables are
    err := db.AutoMigrate(&Order{}, OrderItem{})   ⬅——— created correctly.
    if err != nil {
        return nil, fmt.Errorf("db migration error: %v", err)
    }
    return &Adapter{db: db}, nil
}
```

The NewAdapter function creates an Adapter instance that we can use internally. It is important to understand how the Adapter instance is delegated to functions via receiver functions. For example, to get Order information, we can query the database using the Adapter instance and return it after converting it to a domain model the application can understand. Using the same notation, we can accept the Order domain model as a parameter, transform it to a DB entity, and save the order information in the database. You can see the Get and Save methods in the following two code snippets:

```
func (a Adapter) Get(id string) (domain.Order, error) {        ◁─────  The Get method returns
    var orderEntity Order                                              the domain.Order core
    res := a.db.First(&orderEntity, id)      ▷                         model.
    var orderItems []domain.OrderItem
    for _, orderItem := range orderEntity.OrderItems {        ◁─────
        orderItems = append(orderItems, domain.OrderItem{              Converts Order Items
            ProductCode: orderItem.ProductCode,
            UnitPrice:   orderItem.UnitPrice,
            Quantity:    orderItem.Quantity,
        })
    }
    order := domain.Order{                 ◁───────  Converts Order
        ID:         int64(orderEntity.ID),
        CustomerID: orderEntity.CustomerID,
        Status:     orderEntity.Status,
        OrderItems: orderItems,
        CreatedAt:  orderEntity.CreatedAt.UnixNano(),
    }
    return order, res.Error
}

func (a Adapter) Save(order *domain.Order) error {        ◁──┐   Accepts the domain.Order
    var orderItems []OrderItem                                 │   core model
    for _, orderItem := range order.OrderItems {        ◁──────  Converts Order Items
        orderItems = append(orderItems, OrderItem{
            ProductCode: orderItem.ProductCode,
            UnitPrice:   orderItem.UnitPrice,
            Quantity:    orderItem.Quantity,
        })
    }
    orderModel := Order{                 ◁───────  Converts Order
        CustomerID: order.CustomerID,
        Status:     order.Status,
        OrderItems: orderItems,
    }                                              Saves data into
    res := a.db.Create(&orderModel)      ◁───────  the database
    if res.Error == nil {
        order.ID = int64(orderModel.ID)
    }
    return res.Error
}
```

Finds by ID and puts it into orderEntity

`Get` and `Save` methods reference `Adapter` via receiver functions, and those methods can access DB dependency to write/read order information. Now that we understand how a DB adapter is implemented to save and get order information in this application, let's look at how to introduce gRPC as another adapter.

### 4.2.6 *Implementing a gRPC adapter*

The primary motivation for implementing a gRPC adapter is to provide an interface for the end user to use order functionalities. This interface contains request and response objects that are used during data exchange. The protocol buffer compiler generates request objects, response objects, and service communication layer implementations.

The order module for Golang is in github.com/huseyinbabal/microservices-proto/ golang/order. In previous chapters, we mentioned maintaining .proto files and their generations in a separate repository, and now we will depend on that repository to fulfill the gRPC server. Be careful about using the GitHub username; you need to replace it with yours if you are maintaining .proto files on your own.

The gRPC server adapter depends on `APIPort`, which contains the core functionalities' application module contract. It also depends on gRPC internals generated within the github.com/huseyinbabal/microservices-proto/golang/order repository, which mostly provides forward compatibility. The following code demonstrates this:

**Port to serve gRPC on**
```
type Adapter struct {
    api  ports.APIPort      <──── Core application dependency
    port int
    order.UnimplementedOrderServer    <──── Forward compatibility support
}
```

We can use the same notation to create an adapter for the gRPC server:

```
func NewAdapter(api ports.APIPort, port int) *Adapter {
    return &Adapter{api: api, port: port}
}
```

Now that we've defined the gRPC server adapter and created an instance, let's see how to run this server. The gRPC server requires a socket to listen for requests from clients. To test the gRPC interface, we will perform requests via `grpcurl` (https://github.com/ fullstorydev/grpcurl), a command-line application that helps you easily send gRPC requests by testing gRPC endpoints, something we do mostly with cURL and http endpoints. This is possible if you enable reflection on the server side or if you need to tell `grpcurl` about the location of the .proto files you use in your request. Here's the running logic for a simple gRPC server:

```
func (a Adapter) Run() {
    var err error

    listen, err := net.Listen("tcp", fmt.Sprintf(":%d", a.port))
    if err != nil {
        log.Fatalf("failed to listen on port %d, error: %v", a.port, err)
    }

    grpcServer := grpc.NewServer()
    order.RegisterOrderServer(grpcServer, a)    <──  This method is
    if config.GetEnv() == "development" {   <──      autogenerated by protoc.
        reflection.Register(grpcServer)          Enables reflection
    }                                            to make grpcurl

    if err := grpcServer.Serve(listen); err != nil {
        log.Fatalf("failed to serve grpc on port ")
    }

}
```

This example simply creates a gRPC server that you can make gRPC calls against to handle order-related operations.

Thus far, we've managed to run the gRPC server, but no endpoint has been enabled. To introduce the `Create` endpoint support, we accept the `CreateOrder` request from the end user and process it. This creates a new order out of the gRPC request and uses the `PlaceOrder` function from `APIPort`:

```
func (a Adapter) Create(ctx context.Context, request          ◄── CreateOrderRequest is
    *order.CreateOrderRequest) (*order.CreateOrderResponse, error) {   generated from proto.
    var orderItems []domain.OrderItem
    for _, orderItem := range request.OrderItems {      ◄──
        orderItems = append(orderItems, domain.OrderItem{      Converts OrderItems
            ProductCode: orderItem.ProductCode,                to create a new order
            UnitPrice:   orderItem.UnitPrice,
            Quantity:    orderItem.Quantity,
        })
    }                                                       Creates a new order
    newOrder := domain.NewOrder(request.UserId, orderItems)  ◄── domain object
    result, err := a.api.PlaceOrder(newOrder)   ◄──
    if err != nil {                               Places order via APIPort
        return nil, err
    }
    return &order.CreateOrderResponse{OrderId: result.ID}, nil
}
```

To apply gRPC support, you can start creating the necessary files: touch internal/ adapters/grpc/grpc.go and touch internal/adapters/grpc/server.go.

grpc.go is for defining the handlers, and server.go mostly runs the server and register endpoints inside the grpc.go file. To be able to use the request-response object for the gRPC application, we need to download and add a dependency to the order application by running it in the order service root folder:

```
go get github.com/huseyinbabal/microservices-proto/golang/order
```

Now we are ready to use gRPC models for the `Create` endpoint by adding the following code to the grpc.go file:

```
package grpc

import (
    "context"
    "github.com/huseyinbabal/microservices-proto/golang/order"
    "github.com/huseyinbabal/microservices/order/internal/application/core/
    ➥ domain"
)

func (a Adapter) Create(ctx context.Context, request
➥ *order.CreateOrderRequest) (*order.CreateOrderResponse, error) {
    var orderItems []domain.OrderItem
    for _, orderItem := range request.OrderItems {
```

```
        orderItems = append(orderItems, domain.OrderItem{
            ProductCode: orderItem.ProductCode,
            UnitPrice:   orderItem.UnitPrice,
            Quantity:    orderItem.Quantity,
        })
    }
    newOrder := domain.NewOrder(request.UserId, orderItems)
    result, err := a.api.PlaceOrder(newOrder)
    if err != nil {
        return nil, err
    }
    return &order.CreateOrderResponse{OrderId: result.ID}, nil
}
```

The `Create` method accepts an order creation request from the client, converts it to
the `Order` domain model, and calls `PlaceOrder` via `api` dependency. As a final step, the
following code creates a listener socket and runs the gRPC server. This will also let the
consumer call the `Create` endpoint for order creation. You can simply add it to
server.go:

```
package grpc

import (
    "fmt"
    "github.com/huseyinbabal/microservices-proto/golang/order"   ◁────   Order service
                                                                          golang objects
    "github.com/huseyinbabal/microservices/order/config"   ◁────
    "github.com/huseyinbabal/microservices/order/internal/ports"        Another
    "google.golang.org/grpc/reflection"   ◁────                         package that
    "log"                                     Reflection                 contains app
    "net"                                     to perform                 configs
                                              grpcurl
    "google.golang.org/grpc"
)

type Adapter struct {
    api  ports.APIPort
    port int
    order.UnimplementedOrderServer
}

func NewAdapter(api ports.APIPort, port int) *Adapter {
    return &Adapter{api: api, port: port}
}

func (a Adapter) Run() {
    var err error

    listen, err := net.Listen("tcp", fmt.Sprintf(":%d", a.port))
    if err != nil {
        log.Fatalf("failed to listen on port %d, error: %v", a.port, err)
    }

    grpcServer := grpc.NewServer()
```

```
order.RegisterOrderServer(grpcServer, a)
if config.GetEnv() == "development" {
    reflection.Register(grpcServer)
}

if err := grpcServer.Serve(listen); err != nil {
    log.Fatalf("failed to serve grpc on port ")
}

}
```

Now that we understand ports and adapters in hexagonal architecture, let's look at how to combine them all via dependency injection and then run the application.

### 4.2.7 Dependency injection and running the application

The *12-factor app* is a methodology for building applications that encourages you to

- Use a declarative setup for infrastructure and for application environment automation to quickly deploy to any environment, such as dev, staging, or prod
- Have a clean contract between underlying operating systems so that the same application can be executed on any environment with different parameters
- Use continuous deployment to minimize divergence between environments
- Scale easily without any significant change in the system.

Automation will be addressed in upcoming chapters; the contract between underlying operating systems is the key topic for our current use case. To understand what configuration parameters are available, let's create a config package and implement configuration logic. This is typical configuration management for applications, and in this example, we will do it through environment variables, as suggested in the 12-factor app (https://12factor.net/config).

In the touch config/config.go file, the main logic in the config.go file will expose environment variable values to developers via functions. The order application needs the following environment variables to function properly:

- ENV—This is for separating the prod and non-prod environments. For example, you can enable a debug-level log for non-prod environments and have an info level on the prod environment.
- DATA_SOURCE_URL—This refers to the database connection URL.
- APPLICATION_PORT—This is the port on which the Order service will be served.

The application will fail to start if there is a missing environment variable. Making the application fail fast due to a missing configuration is better than silently allowing it to start, which might cause major inconsistencies due to empty environment variable values (e.g., empty API_URL). We can use the following implementation to properly address these concerns and read environment variable values:

```
package config

import (
    "log"
    "os"
    "strconv"
)

func GetEnv() string {
    return getEnvironmentValue("ENV")          Possible values for
}                                              development/production

func GetDataSourceURL() string {
    return getEnvironmentValue("DATA_SOURCE_URL")    Database connection URL
}

func GetApplicationPort() int {
    portStr := getEnvironmentValue("APPLICATION_PORT")    Order service port
    port, err := strconv.Atoi(portStr)

    if err != nil {
        log.Fatalf("port: %s is invalid", portStr)
    }

    return port
}
func getEnvironmentValue(key string) string {    GetEnv returns the string.
    if os.Getenv(key) == "" {
        log.Fatalf("%s environment variable is missing.", key)
    }

    return os.Getenv(key)
}
```

This is an example of reading an environment variable from which you can get a value or error. Now we are ready to get the configuration through environment variables; that means we can prepare adapters and plug them into application ports. Let's create our application endpoint with the following command:

```
touch cmd/main.go
```

The DB adapter needs a data source URL to connect and return an instance for a DB reference. The core application needs this DB adaptor to modify order objects in the database. Finally, the gRPC adapter needs a core application and a specific port to get the gRPC up and running via the Run method:

```
package main

import (
    "github.com/huseyinbabal/microservices/order/config"
    "github.com/huseyinbabal/microservices/order/internal/adapters/db"
    "github.com/huseyinbabal/microservices/order/internal/adapters/grpc"
```

```
        "github.com/huseyinbabal/microservices/order/internal/application/core/
        ➥ api"
        "log"
)

func main() {
    dbAdapter, err := db.NewAdapter(config.GetDataSourceURL())
    if err != nil {
        log.Fatalf("Failed to connect to database. Error: %v", err)
    }

    application := api.NewApplication(dbAdapter)
    grpcAdapter := grpc.NewAdapter(application, config.GetApplicationPort())
    grpcAdapter.Run()
}
```

As you can see, the gRPC needs a database, which is MySQL. Docker (https://www.docker.com/), an OS-level virtualization to deliver software in containers, can help us quickly run a MySQL database with a predefined database and user:

```
docker run -p 3306:3306 \
    -e MYSQL_ROOT_PASSWORD=verysecretpass \
    -e MYSQL_DATABASE=order mysql
```

In this case, our data source URL is

```
root:verysecretpass@tcp(127.0.0.1:3306)/order
```

To run the Order service application, you can use the following:

```
DATA_SOURCE_URL=root:verysecretpass@tcp(127.0.0.1:3306)/order \
APPLICATION_PORT=3000 \
ENV=development \
go run cmd/main.go
```

If you get dependency errors, you can execute `go mod tidy` to reorganize dependencies and rerun the application. Now that we understand how to run an application, let's look at a running gRPC service.

### 4.2.8   Calling a gRPC endpoint

The `Order` application has the Order service and `Create rpc` inside it. To send a `CreateOrder` request, you can pass `CreateOrderRequest` as a JSON to `grpcurl`:

```
grpcurl -d '{"user_id": 123, "order_items": [{"product_code": "prod",
➥ "quantity": 4, "unit_price": 12}]}' -plaintext localhost:3000
➥ Order/Create 0
```

This is similar to cURL, which accepts a request payload with a `-d` parameter. The `-plaintext` parameter is used to disable TLS during gRPC communication. The Order service will return a response after a successful request:

```
{
  "orderId": "1"
}
```

This is a simple response, but we will see advanced scenarios and proper exception-handling mechanisms in upcoming chapters.

## Summary

- Hexagonal architecture helps you isolate layers in your microservice to implement testable and clean applications.
- Ports are used for defining contracts between layers, while adapters are concrete implementations that can be plugged into ports to make the core application available to the end user.
- Implementing the application core first and then continuing with the outer layers is helpful.
- GORM is an ORM library for Go with good abstraction for database-related operations.
- Twelve-factor applications have good use cases for microservices in that application configurations can be passed through environment variables and that you can configure them based on the environment.
- Combining layers in hexagonal architecture is done with dependency injection.
- `grpcurl` provides a cURL-like behavior to handle order data by calling gRPC endpoints.

# Interservice communication

**This chapter covers**

- Understanding the internals of gRPC client-server connection strategies
- How to depend on a client module to access a specific service
- Tips and tricks for client configuration of a particular service
- Handling errors

In the previous chapter, we implemented a gRPC service for the Order service. In this chapter, we will implement a gRPC client for that service to show how underlying communication works in microservice architecture. You can see the high-level picture of interservice communication in figure 5.1.

In previous chapters, we saw how to generate Go source codes from proto files; now, we will learn how to use repositories that contain gRPC stubs as Go module dependencies on the client side. gRPC also provides flexible configurations for client connections to make interservice communication more reliable. These configurations

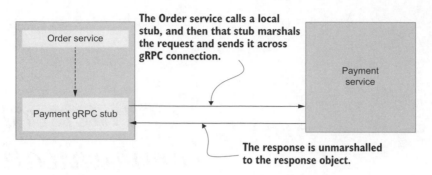

**Figure 5.1   The Order service uses a Payment service gRPC stub.**

allow us to retry operations based on the response status or error type we get from the gRPC response. Let's look at an example to better understand how communication works and how we can handle error cases to have a better failover strategy.

## 5.1   gRPC service-to-service communication

In a distributed microservice architecture, a service may have multiple identical backends to handle a certain consumer load. Those backends have a discrete capacity, and loads from clients are distributed using load balancers. For example, saying "Call Payment service from Order service" does not mean we connect an endpoint that contains just one instance. This type of connection is called *server-side load balancing*: the client connects to a single endpoint, and that endpoint proxies requests to backend instances. Alternatively, the client may want to be able to connect multiple backends explicitly for the Payment service. This type of connection is called *client-side load balancing*.

We will use Kubernetes in upcoming chapters to handle our microservices in a containerization environment. Kubernetes provides an out-of-the-box solution for service communication, and we will use server-side load balancing. Now that we understand the initial concepts of client- and server-side load balancing, let's take a detailed look at the characteristics of these strategies.

### 5.1.1   Server-side load balancing

In server-side load balancing, the client makes an RPC call to a load balancer (or proxy). The load balancer distributes the RPC call to one of the available application instances (e.g., the Payment service), as shown in figure 5.2. The load balancer also tracks the load status of each instance to distribute the load fairly. The client application is not aware of actual backend instances for server-side load balancing.

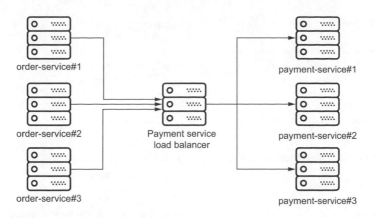

**Figure 5.2** Server-side load balancing: the Order service calls the Payment service load balancer, and that load balancer proxies requests to backend instances.

### 5.1.2 Client-side load balancing

There are different kinds of load balancing algorithms (http://mng.bz/rWVB), and with minimum configuration, the client can ignore the load report and use a *round-robin algorithm* in which traffic is distributed to backend instances in rotation. In client-side load balancing, the client knows the addresses of multiple backend instances of an application and chooses one of the available instances to make an RPC call. The client collects insights from backend instances to decide which backend service to call for fair distribution. In an ideal scenario, the client makes an RPC call to the backend instance, and the instance returns its load report so that the client can decide on instance selection (see figure 5.3).

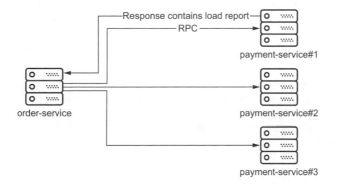

**Figure 5.3** Client-side load balancing: the client is aware of backend instances, and it knows on which instance the next RPC call should be performed from the load report.

Table 5.1 summarizes the pros and cons of load-balancing strategies.

**Table 5.1  Server-side LB versus client-side LB**

|  | Server-side LB | Client-side LB |
|---|---|---|
| **Pros** | Easy to configure | Better performance since there is no extra hop |
|  | The client does not need to know backends | No single point of failure |
| **Cons** | More latency | Hard to configure |
|  | Limited throughput may affect scalability | Tracks instance health and load |
|  |  | Language-specific implementations |

Now that we understand the load balancer options for service communication, let's look at how to use payment service stubs in the Order service.

## 5.2   Depending on a module and implementing ports and adapters

In Go, package names are mostly structured around a version control system URL, such as GitHub. You must use your account and replace the username in import statements for dependency packages. For example, feel free to replace import `"github.com/huseyinbabal/ microservices/order/internal/application/core/domain"` with import `"github.com/<your_ user_name>/microservices/order/internal/application/core/domain"`.

We described how to generate Go service source code out of .proto files and auto-mated it within GitHub Actions in chapter 3. Those generated source files contain stubs for gRPC clients to call methods defined by the service. For example, the Order service, which we implemented in chapter 4, depends on the Payment service to charge the customer for specified order items. The Order service should include Payment service stubs to call the `Create` method on the Payment service. You can simply run the following command to add a payment module to the Order service project:

```
go get -u github.com/huseyinbabal/microservices-proto/golang/payment
```

This command will always download the latest version of the module, but you can also depend on a specific version to prevent unexpected behaviors like this:

```
go get -u github.com/huseyinbabal/microservices-
➡ proto/golang/payment@v1.0.38
```

This will fix the version of the payment module dependency so that you always get the same version whenever you refresh your dependencies. After you add the Payment service dependency to the Order service, you can use the following code to call the Payment service:

```
paymentClient := payment.NewPaymentClient(conn, opts)
paymentClient.Create(ctx, &CreatePaymentRequest{})
```

The primary motivation for creating a payment client is fulfilling the Order service's goal: charge customers when they try to place an order. Now that we have seen a quick summary of how the Order service will use a payment client, let's look at the implementation details of integrating the Payment service into the Order service.

### 5.2.1   *Payment port*

As discussed in chapter 4, a port is an interface that contains contracts about a business model in hexagonal architecture. When we say "port," we mean the contract of a payment operation or a Go interface that contains payment-related function signatures, not the concrete implementation of a specific payment strategy. The main expectation from the payment port is adding the capability of inserting a payment step within the Order creation flow. This way, the Order service will never depend on a concrete implementation but on an interface. Because the Order service uses this payment port, this is located on the driven side of hexagonal architecture, as shown in figure 5.4.

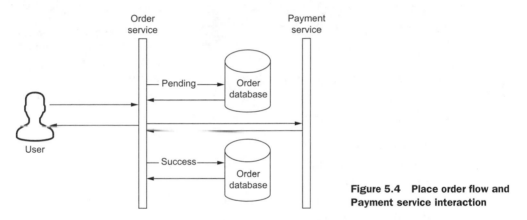

**Figure 5.4   Place order flow and Payment service interaction**

### 5.2.2   *Payment adapter*

There can be multiple implementations of payment ports, called adapters. If your adapter implementation is suitable for a payment port contract and contains identical function signatures with the port interface, you can easily plug that adapter into the payment port. This is done by dependency injection: you have the actual implementation of the payment port, and you simply initialize and add it to the `Order` domain model during application initialization to call it during the payment step.

We should have a payment port and adapter in the Order service to interact with the Payment service, as shown in figure 5.5. If we clearly state those components in the hexagon, the picture and design of the Order service based on those components are more visible.

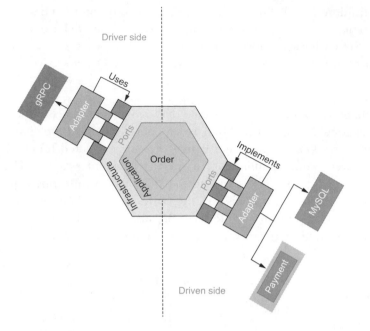

**Figure 5.5   Port and adapter for a payment stub**

Now that we understand how the Order service evolves with the payment module, let's zoom into the payment port and adapter and review step-by-step explanations on how to implement a payment strategy for the Order service.

### 5.2.3   *Implementing the payment port*

The payment port allows the Order service to call the Payment service (http://mng.bz/V1xP). To define a basic contract in a payment port, you can simply go to the Order service project we implemented in chapter 4 and create a payment port file: mkdir -p internal/ports && touch internal/ports/payment.go.

The payment port has only one functionality: charge. Simply pass the actual order object, and it charges the customer based on order details:

```
package ports

import "github.com/huseyinbabal/microservices/order/internal/application/
➡ core/domain"

type PaymentPort interface {
    Charge(*domain.Order) error
}
```

Now that we have PaymentPort, let's see what the payment adapter looks like.

### 5.2.4   *Implementing the payment adapter*

The primary motivation behind the payment adapter is to help the Order service access the Payment service to charge the customer. The payment adapter will depend on a payment stub from autogenerated source code managed in a separate repo (http://mng.bz/x42W; you can see the details in chapter 3). Simply call a function locally with a payment stub that runs on the remote server, the Payment service. This stub implementation is about marshalling requests on the client side (Order service), sending them through gRPC, then unmarshalling requests on the server side (Payment service) to call the actual function (figure 5.6).

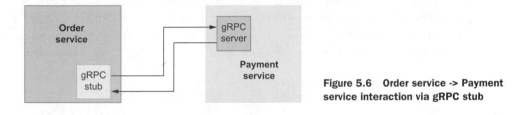

**Figure 5.6   Order service -> Payment service interaction via gRPC stub**

Let's create an adapter file to add concrete payment stub implementations: mkdir -p internal/adapters/payment && touch internal/adapters/payment/payment.go. Since the payment adapter depends on the payment stub from the autogenerated Go source code, its structure will look like the following in payment.go:

```
package payment

import (
    "context"
    "github.com/huseyinbabal/microservices-proto/golang/payment"
    "github.com/huseyinbabal/microservices/order/internal/application/core/
        ➥ domain"
    "google.golang.org/grpc"
    "google.golang.org/grpc/credentials/insecure"
)

type Adapter struct {
    payment payment.PaymentClient          ⇐──┐ This comes from
}                                              generated Go source.
```

Notice that the payment adapter is responsible for handling payment-related operations, and the Order service does not need to know these internals. The next step is to provide an initialization method to create a new adapter, like the one that follows, and you can append it to the payment.go file:

```
func NewAdapter(paymentServiceUrl string) (*Adapter, error) {        Data model
    var opts []grpc.DialOption          ⇐──────────────┐            for connection
    opts = append(opts,                                              configurations
➥      grpc.WithTransportCredentials(insecure.NewCredentials()))    Connects
    conn, err := grpc.Dial(paymentServiceUrl, opts...)   ⇐────────── to service
```

This is for disabling TLS.

```
if err != nil {
    return nil, err
}
defer conn.Close()
client := payment.NewPaymentClient(conn)
return &Adapter{payment: client}, nil
}
```

Always close the connection before quitting the function.

Initializes the new payment stub instance

grpc.WithTransportCredentials(insecure.NewCredentials()) means disabling the TLS handshake during client-server connection. This is for simplifying the explanation of concepts, but we will dive deep into TLS-enabled connections in future chapters. Finally, we can implement the Charge method to satisfy the contract of the payment port using a payment stub: we can simply call the Create method through paymentClient, which is already injected in the payment adapter. Refer to the following implementation for simple payment creation using the order object in payment.go:

```
func (a *Adapter) Charge(order *domain.Order) error {
    _, err := a.payment.Create(context.Background(),
     &payment.CreatePaymentRequest{
        UserId:     order.CustomerID,
        OrderId:    order.ID,
        TotalPrice: order.TotalPrice(),
    })
    return err
}
```

This request comes from an autogenerated Go code.

TotalPrice is calculated from order details, as follows:

```
func (o *Order) TotalPrice() float32 {
    var totalPrice float32
    for _, orderItem := range o.OrderItems {
        totalPrice += orderItem.UnitPrice * float32(orderItem.Quantity)
    }
    return totalPrice
}
```

For now, ignore the error handling part in this example, but we will get back to error handling soon. Let's look at how we can provide configuration to the payment client so that it can request that endpoint.

### 5.2.5 *Client configuration for a payment stub*

In previous chapters, we set up a configuration system to access the specific configurations needed by the Order service. We need a payment service endpoint (or URL) for a payment stub to use, and the following function is a good candidate for resolving that:

```
func GetPaymentServiceUrl() string {
    return getEnvironmentValue("PAYMENT_SERVICE_URL")
}

func getEnvironmentValue(key string) string {
```

This will be in the Order service env params.

Validates env param exists and gets it

```
    if os.Getenv(key) == "" {
        log.Fatalf("%s environment variable is missing.", key)
    }

    return os.Getenv(key)
}
```

We assume that the value of PAYMENT_SERVICE_URL is somehow known for now, but we will see the internals of how to auto-discover the payment endpoint in chapter 8. Since we know how to get the payment endpoint, we can use the following code to initialize the payment adapter for the Order service:

**The payment endpoint is available on the config object.**

```
paymentAdapter, err := payment.NewAdapter(config.GetPaymentServiceUrl())   ◁───┘
if err != nil {
        log.Fatalf("Failed to initialize payment stub. Error: %v", err)   ◁───
}
```

**The Order service will not run without the payment config.**

The Order service needs this payment adapter to create an order successfully. To inject a payment adapter to the Order service, we can use following code within main.go:

```
func main() {
    dbAdapter, err := db.NewAdapter(config.GetDataSourceURL())
    if err != nil {
        log.Fatalf("Failed to connect to database. Error: %v", err)
    }

    paymentAdapter, err :=
    ▶ payment.NewAdapter(config.GetPaymentServiceUrl())
    if err != nil {
        log.Fatalf("Failed to initialize payment stub. Error: %v", err)
    }

    application := api.NewApplication(dbAdapter, paymentAdapter)   ◁───┐
    grpcAdapter := grpc.NewAdapter(application,       The payment adapter is now a
    ▶ config.GetApplicationPort())                    must-have parameter.
    grpcAdapter.Run()
}
```

As always, main.go is the place where we handle dependency injections. We create a payment and DB adapter and pass them to the Order service. Now that we understand how to implement and use a payment adapter to inject it into the Order service, let's look at how we can make it available in the gRPC endpoint within order creation.

### 5.2.6   *Using a payment adapter in gRPC*

gRPC is one of the adapters in the Order service, as you can see in the internal/adapters/grpc package. The gRPC adapter depends on APIPort, which is the core of the Order service:

```
type Adapter struct {
    api  ports.APIPort        ◁———— This contains the payment adapter.
    port int
    order.UnimplementedOrderServer
}

func NewAdapter(api ports.APIPort, port int) *Adapter {
    return &Adapter{api: api, port: port}
}
```

When you check the `APIPort` interface, you see it contains the payment adapter we implemented in this chapter. In the current implementation of order creation, the `Create` endpoint calls the `PlaceOrder` method of the `APIPort`:

```
func (a Adapter) Create(ctx context.Context, request
⇒ *order.CreateOrderRequest) (*order.CreateOrderResponse, error) {
    var orderItems []domain.OrderItem
    for _, orderItem := range request.OrderItems {
        orderItems = append(orderItems, domain.OrderItem{
            ProductCode: orderItem.ProductCode,
            UnitPrice:   orderItem.UnitPrice,
            Quantity:    orderItem.Quantity,
        })
    }
    newOrder := domain.NewOrder(request.UserId, orderItems)
    result, err := a.api.PlaceOrder(newOrder)    ◁———┐
    if err != nil {                                  │ The API knows how to
        return nil, err                              │ use a payment adapter.
    }
    return &order.CreateOrderResponse{OrderId: result.ID}, nil
}
```

Once you go to the `PlaceOrder` method in internal/application/core/api/api.go, it saves order requests into the database with the `PENDING` state:

```
func (a Application) PlaceOrder(order domain.Order) (domain.Order, error) {
    err := a.db.Save(&order)
    if err != nil {
        return domain.Order{}, err
    }
    return order, nil
}
```

Now we add another step: calling the Payment service to charge the customer for that specific order:

```
func (a Application) PlaceOrder(order domain.Order) (domain.Order, error) {
    err := a.db.Save(&order)
    if err != nil {
        return domain.Order{}, err
    }
    paymentErr := a.payment.Charge(&order)    ◁———— Charges for the current order
```

```
    if paymentErr != nil {
        return domain.Order{}, paymentErr
    }
    return order, nil
}
```

Now that we understand how to call the Payment service within the gRPC endpoint, let's look at how we can handle errors to decide on the next step of retrying or marking the operation as failed. As you can see, we call the Payment service, and for a specific reason: it may return an error. In the example, we return that error to the client side directly, but it is better to differentiate errors to take different actions on the client side.

## 5.3 Error handling

Thus far, we have assumed that everything went well during service-to-service communication, which means the server returned an OK status message to the client. However, in real-life applications, there can be problems during service communication, and you need to understand what happened in these cases. If an error occurs, gRPC returns two basic pieces of information: a *status code* and an *optional error message* that explains the problem in detail. Let's look at some of the status codes and their use cases.

### 5.3.1 Status codes

gRPC uses predefined status codes within the RPC protocol that are understood among different languages. For example, for successful operations, gRPC returns an OK status code. All the remaining codes are about unsuccessful use cases:

- CANCELLED—In this use case, the client calls the server, and for a specific reason, it cancels the request. For example, you call multiple services, and for whichever returns first, you use that data and cancel the other requests.
- INVALID_ARGUMENT—This status code is caused by the caller in that it provides invalid input, and the server complains about that. For example, the server will return this status code if you provide an empty order ID during payment creation.
- DEADLINE_EXCEEDED—This status code shows that the deadline expired before the actual operation could complete. For example, say you configure your client to have a deadline of 5 seconds. If you call an endpoint with this client and it takes 6 seconds to complete, you will see it will get DEADLINE_EXCEEDED after 5 seconds before the actual operation finishes.
- NOT_FOUND—This status code states that a resource is not found. For example, you want to get order details by ID, but you get NOT_FOUND since there is no order with that ID.
- ALREADY_EXISTS—This status code is for preventing resource duplication. For example, if you try creating a user with an existing email address, the server will return this status code.

- PERMISSION_DENIED—If the operation is not allowed for the current caller, the server will return this status code. You might be already logged into the system, but the resource you are trying to access may need higher permissions.
- RESOURCE_EXHAUSTED—This code is used once the caller reaches its limit for usage. For example, you may have a quota for a Software as a Service (SaaS) product; then, once you reach the limit for the product in that environment, the server will return this status code.
- INTERNAL—This status code is used for internal server errors.

(See the gRPC status codes here: http://mng.bz/Aodz.) Now that we understand the meanings of gRPC status codes, let's look at how we can use them in gRPC responses.

### 5.3.2   *Returning an error code and message*

Consider the following code from the Payment service to better understand the error structure:

```
func (a Adapter) Create(ctx context.Context, request
    *payment.CreatePaymentRequest) (*payment.CreatePaymentResponse, error) {
    newPayment := domain.NewPayment(request.UserId, request.OrderId,
        request.TotalPrice)
    result, err := a.api.Charge(newPayment)         Assume this returns an error.
    // Assume it returns something like => err = errors.New("failed to
        charge customer")
    if err != nil {
        return nil, err
    }
    return &payment.CreatePaymentResponse{PaymentId: result.ID}, nil
}
```

If you call the Create endpoint of the Payment service with the following command, the result will create a clear picture:

```
grpcurl -d '{"user_id": 123, "order_id":12, "total_price": 32}' -plaintext
    localhost:3001 Payment/Create
ERROR:
  Code: Unknown
  Message: failed to charge the customer
```

As you can see, the Message field is there, but what about the code field? That is missing because we simply returned an error object instead of gRPC status. Let's refine the code a bit so that it also returns code:

```
func (a Adapter) Create(ctx context.Context, request
    *payment.CreatePaymentRequest) (*payment.CreatePaymentResponse, error) {
    newPayment := domain.NewPayment(request.UserId, request.OrderId,
        request.TotalPrice)
    result, err := a.api.Charge(newPayment)    Assume this returns an error.
    // Assume it returns => err = status.Errorf(
        codes.InvalidArgument,
```

```
    fmt.Sprintf("failed to charge user: %d", request.UserId))
    if err != nil {
        return nil, err
    }
    return &payment.CreatePaymentResponse{PaymentId: result.ID}, nil
}
```

Once we make another payment `Create` endpoint call, you will see the following response:

```
grpcurl -d '{"user_id": 123, "order_id":12, "total_price": 32}' -plaintext
⮕ localhost:3001 Payment/Create
ERROR:
  Code: InvalidArgument
  Message: failed to charge user: 123
```

Error codes help you understand the error category and decide on the next step. Now that we know how to return errors with their statuses and codes, let's try to add more details to those errors for a better understanding of the root cause of the problem.

### 5.3.3 Errors with details

In the previous example, we assumed that the customer's credit card failed to charge, and, in this case, we should propagate this error to the Order service to let it return a proper message to the consumer. Since the Order service depends on multiple services, such as the Payment and Shipping services, any error can be caused by several reasons: insufficient balance, invalid shipping address, and so on. The gRPC status package has another constructor to allow passing more details to the status object. The following code is a good example for explaining why the order creation failed:

```
func (a Application) PlaceOrder(order domain.Order) (domain.Order, error) {
    err := a.db.Save(&order)
    if err != nil {
        return domain.Order{}, err
    }
    paymentErr := a.payment.Charge(&order)         Resolves status from
    if paymentErr != nil {                          a payment error
        st, _ := status.FromError(paymentErr)  ◄──┘
        fieldErr := &errdetails.BadRequest_FieldViolation{
            Field:       "payment",
            Description: st.Message(),                        Populates with an
        }                                                    actual payment detail
        badReq := &errdetails.BadRequest{}
        badReq.FieldViolations = append(badReq.FieldViolations, fieldErr) ◄──┘
        orderStatus := status.New(codes.InvalidArgument, "order creation
        ⮕ failed")            ◄──── Creates the root status
        statusWithDetails, _ := orderStatus.WithDetails(badReq) ◄──
        return domain.Order{}, statusWithDetails.Err()          Augments
    }                                                           the status
    return order, nil                                           with a
}                                                               payment
                                                                error
```

Annotations: **Payment error as a separate field** | **Initiates a bad request error**

Here, we reuse the error from the Payment service and return the new error from the Order service. If you make another call to create an endpoint from the Payment service, you will get following:

```
grpcurl -d '{"user_id": 123, "order_items":[{"product_code":"sku1",
➥ "unit_price": 0.12, "quantity":1}]}' -plaintext localhost:3000
➥ Order/Create
ERROR:
  Code: InvalidArgument
  Message: order creation failed
  Details:
  1)
      {"@type":"type.googleapis.com/google.rpc.BadRequest","fieldViolations":
      ➥ [{"field":"payment","description":"failed to charge. invalid billing
      ➥ address "}]}
```

As you can see, the error structure iteratively stays refactored so that those messages can be propagated to the user. Now that we know how to return more detailed status objects from a gRPC endpoint, let's look at how we can handle those messages on the client side.

### 5.3.4   *Handling errors on the client side*

In our examples, the Order service is a Payment service client because it charges users for specific orders. If a problem occurs during a charge operation, the Payment service returns an error, and the Order Service should understand what happened to the operation. In a typical status response, there can be an error and a message to explain what happened. To handle this status on the client side, the gRPC status package provides a function to resolve the status from the error. The `PlaceOrder` endpoint of the Order service would get an error from the Payment service `Create` endpoint. In this case, we can resolve the status object from the error object. Since any gRPC service may call multiple services to aggregate data, it is also valuable to group errors to understand the source of the error in the response:

```
func (a Application) PlaceOrder(order domain.Order) (domain.Order, error) {
    err := a.db.Save(&order)
    if err != nil {
        return domain.Order{}, err
    }
    paymentErr := a.payment.Charge(&order)        Status object from
    if paymentErr != nil {                        a payment error
        st, _ := status.FromError(paymentErr)   ◁─┘
        fieldErr := &errdetails.BadRequest_FieldViolation{
            Field:        "payment",
            Description:  st.Message(),
        }
        badReq := &errdetails.BadRequest{}
        badReq.FieldViolations = append(badReq.FieldViolations, fieldErr)
        orderStatus := status.New(codes.InvalidArgument, "order creation
        ➥ failed")
```

Annotations:
- **Payment error section** points to the `fieldErr := &errdetails.BadRequest_FieldViolation{ ... }` block
- **Root error** points to the `orderStatus := status.New(codes.InvalidArgument, "order creation failed")` block

```
        statusWithDetails, _ := orderStatus.WithDetails(badReq)    ◁──┐  Populates
        return domain.Order{}, statusWithDetails.Err()                │  with a
    }                                                                 │  payment
    return order, nil                                                 │  error
}
```

This example assumes the Payment service returns a simple status object with code and a message, but if it returns the message with details, we may need to extract those field violations separately. In that case, we can use the built-in status.Convert() instead of status.FromError():

```
func (a Application) PlaceOrder(order domain.Order) (domain.Order, error) {
    err := a.db.Save(&order)
    if err != nil {
        return domain.Order{}, err
    }
    paymentErr := a.payment.Charge(&order)
    if paymentErr != nil {                     ┌─  Converts a complex
        st := status.Convert(paymentErr)   ◁──┘   error to a status
        var allErrors []string
        for _, detail := range st.Details() {         ┌─  Used for a Bad
            switch t := detail.(type) {                │   Request case
            case *errdetails.BadRequest:   ◁───────────┘
                for _, violation := range t.GetFieldViolations() {
                    allErrors = append(allErrors, violation.Description)
                }
            }
        }
        fieldErr := &errdetails.BadRequest_FieldViolation{
            Field:       "payment",
            Description: strings.Join(allErrors, "\n"),
        }
        badReq := &errdetails.BadRequest{}
        badReq.FieldViolations = append(badReq.FieldViolations, fieldErr)
        orderStatus := status.New(codes.InvalidArgument, "order creation
          ➡ failed")
        statusWithDetails, _ := orderStatus.WithDetails(badReq)   ◁──┐  Expands
        return domain.Order{}, statusWithDetails.Err()               │  the root
    }                                                                │  error with
    return order, nil                                               │  details
}
```

Annotations: "Slices for whole errors" points to `var allErrors []string`. "Payment errors as fields" points to `}` after `fieldErr`. "A root error on the Order service" points to `failed")`.

During interservice communication, we may not need to convert statuses frequently, but when it comes to software development kits (SDKs), such as a client implementation, your entire application may need to handle those error messages, as shown, to understand what happened in the system and provide a meaningful message to the end user. We've completed all the Payment and Order service steps; now let's see how to run them.

### 5.3.5   *Running the Payment service*

As a reminder, you can access the payment module here: http://mng.bz/V1xP. If you have already cloned the repository, simply go to the payment folder and run the following:

```
DB_DRIVER=mysql \
DATA_SOURCE_URL=root:verysecretpass@tcp(127.0.0.1:3306)/payment \   ⟵── Changes DB
APPLICATION_PORT=3001 \                                                  URL based
ENV=development \                                                        on your
go run cmd/main.go                                                       setup
```

Now the Payment service is available on port 3001. Let's go to the order module and run the Order service with a configuration that also includes the location of the Payment service:

```
DB_DRIVER=mysql \
DATA_SOURCE_URL=root:verysecretpass@tcp(127.0.0.1:3306)/order \   ⟵── Points the DB
APPLICATION_PORT=3000 \                                               URL to running
ENV=development \                           Endpoint for the          a MySQL
PAYMENT_SERVICE_URL=localhost:3001 \   ⟵── Payment service           instance
go run cmd/main.go
```

Now we have two local running services, and we only call the Order service. Once it is needed, the Order service will call the Payment service in the background. In other words, the Payment service is not open to the public since there is no suitable endpoint for the end user, whereas the Order service is open to the end user. The Order service can call the Payment service because they are in the same network.

## *Summary*

- Because the Order service depends on the Payment service, the Payment service can be defined as the outgoing port and adapter within the Order service hexagon.
- If a typical service calls another service, it can use stubs of the other service to initialize and call any endpoint available on the second service.
- A separate repository for .proto files helps us share generated code in services and client SDKs that can be used to generate source code for different services; a service depends on another service's stub to call it.
- In the client-side load-balancing technique, the caller knows the location of the service endpoints; in the server-side load-balancing approach, the caller trusts the server because the server knows the downstream services.
- The status package provides a more structured way than returning pure errors to return the status code and descriptive error message and better understand what happened.

# Resilient communication

**This chapter covers**

- Tips and tricks for how to use retry and timeout for gRPC communication
- Using circuit breakers for interservice communication to have better resiliency
- Error handling during service communications
- Securing interservice communication with TLS configuration

In a typical monolithic application, any critical error can bring the entire system down because all the application components live in one shared runtime. Once you switch to microservice architecture, those components are decoupled by extracting to separate services, but this distributed system environment has its own disadvantages. For this reason, microservices should be designed for resiliency and always be fault tolerant. Let's look at the problematic use cases in a microservices environment first, then explain the possible solutions to make microservices resilient and fault tolerant.

**Using code listings**

Unimportant parts of code are removed from examples in this section. To run any code listing, go to this repository: https://github.com/huseyinbabal/grpc-microservices-in-go/ fork.

1. Go to the GitHub Actions repository you forked on your GitHub account: https:// github.com/<your_username>/grpc-microservices-in-go/actions/workflows/ listing_execute.yaml
2. Click Run Workflow and provide the listing number (e.g., 2.1).
3. You can see all the outputs of execution, especially the Run step that contains code listing output, if there is any.

## 6.1 *Resiliency patterns*

It is possible to have network failures in a distributed system environment, and this can cause a malfunction in a specific service. For example, if the Shipping service cannot access its database due to network failure, it will be out of order after some time. Since the Order service uses the Shipping service to ship orders after successful payment, this database failure will ultimately affect the Order service. Suppose there is no proper resiliency pattern for interservice communication. In that case, it can cause a cascading failure in that the Order service also becomes unreachable, even though it should be able to handle other types of requests that do not depend on the Shipping service. With a proper resiliency pattern, we would time out the shipping operation or apply some logic to fail fast now and retry it in the future once the Shipping service is back.

In figure 6.1, there is a complete network failure in that the Shipping service cannot access the database; it might also be a partial failure in that the network is okay, but there is a latency between the service and database that breaches the service-level objective. Assume that you have a 50 MS average latency limit for your interservice communication, which sometimes exceeds this limit. You can apply resiliency patterns to this use case: once the average request latency exceeds the limit, you halt sending the request for a while and then resume after a specific time. This prevents memory leaks by dropping long-lived connections to other services, which can cause a possible cascading failure. Now that you understand a common example of a failure in a microservice environment, let's look at how we can recover from this state by using patterns such as timeout, retry, and circuit breaker to make communication more resilient.

### 6.1.1 *Timeout pattern*

In a microservice pattern, you have multiple services, and they handle a task together: each service applies its business logic to this task to complete the whole task successfully. For example, the Order service depends on the Payment service to charge customers for their orders, and the Order service depends on the Shipping service to ship the customer order after a successful payment to mark the order creation as successful. Service dependencies like these may lead to bottlenecks or, even worse, single

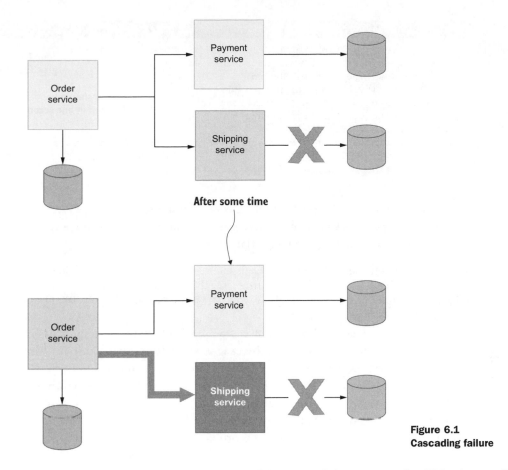

**Figure 6.1
Cascading failure**

points of failure in a microservices architecture. A latency on the Shipping or Payment services can affect the Order service and become very slow. If you have a commitment on the latency numbers, you may need to revisit the network communication logic for those services and apply some timeout pattern to fail fast instead of breaching the latency commitment. Let's look at concrete examples of canceling requests if they take more time than committed latency numbers allow.

As you may remember, once we generate the source code from .proto files, service functions take `context.Context` as the first parameter. This lets users pass their context to a specific service call to control the execution. But what is `context.Context`? The context in Go enables you to specify deadlines, cancellation signals, or key-value pairs available between processes. If you define a context with a deadline specification and pass it to a function, that function should be finished before the deadline; if not, it will be automatically canceled. For example, if we call the Shipping service to ship order items to a customer, you can limit the client side to one second to see the shipping response from the server side.

**Listing 6.1   Timeout pattern on the client side**

```
shippingClient := shipping.NewShippingServiceClient(conn)
  ctx, _ := context.WithDeadline(context.Background(),
    time.Now().Add(1*time.Second))
  log.Println("Creating shipping...")
  _, errCreate := shippingClient.Create(ctx,
    &shipping.CreateShippingRequest{UserId: 23})
  if errCreate != nil {
     log.Printf("Failed to create shipping. Err: %v", errCreate)
  } else {
     log.Println("Shipping is created successfully.")
  }
```

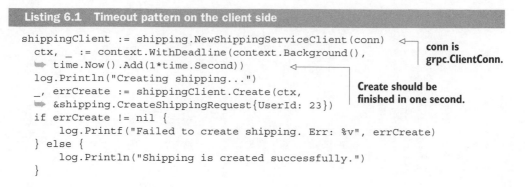

conn is
grpc.ClientConn.

Create should be
finished in one second.

`context.WithDeadline` requires a target date as a parameter, but there is an easier step: `context.WithTimeout`, a wrapper for `WithDeadline` that allows you to specify a timeout value instead of calculating the target date from the current time:

```
ctx, _ := context.WithTimeout(context.Background(), 1*time.Second)
```

Both functions take a parent context, `context.Background()`, which in our case is an empty context without a deadline.

`context.WithTimeout` and `context.WithDeadline` both return two values: `context` and `cancellation` functions. You can call the `cancellation` function to halt any further execution within that context, as needed. More concretely, you can call three competing endpoints with the same context, then cancel the context for the remaining two when the first endpoint finishes and returns a value. This way, you do not have to wait for other endpoint responses that are no longer needed.

Another advantage of using context is propagating context information between services. In gRPC, context is available on both the client and server sides. That means that if there are three services to fulfill an operation, the initial context can be propagated to the final one without extra context definition on the second and third services. For example, I know that the `order` operation should take at most three seconds to complete, and in our scenario, the Order service calls the Payment service, then the Shipping service. We can create a context with a three-second timeout and use it in three services (figure 6.2).

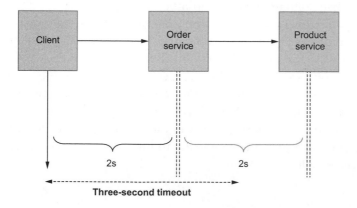

Figure 6.2   Context timeout
propagation from client to the
Order and Product services

The client initializes a context with a timeout value and uses it in further gRPC calls.

**Listing 6.2   Context timeout propagation**

```
...                                                    The Product Service's Get endpoint
func (s *server) Get(ctx context.Context, in *product.GetProductRequest)
    (*product.GetProductResponse, error) {
        time.Sleep(2 * time.Second)                    ◄──────────
        return &product.GetProductResponse{Title: "Demo title"}, nil    Two
}                                                                       seconds delay
...                                                                     simulation.
```

```
...
func (s *server) Create(ctx context.Context, in *order.CreateOrderRequest)
    (*order.CreateOrderResponse, error) {
        time.Sleep(2 * time.Second)          ◄──── Two seconds delay simulation.
        productInfo, err := s.productClient.Get(ctx,
            &product.GetProductRequest{ProductId: in.ProductId})
        if err != nil {
            return nil, err
        }
        return &order.CreateOrderResponse{OrderId: 123, ProductTitle:
            productInfo.Title}, nil
}
...
```

**The Order service's Create endpoint**

```
...
orderServiceClient := order.NewOrderServiceClient(conn)
    ctx, _ := context.WithTimeout(context.TODO(), time.Second*3)    ◄─────
    log.Println("Creating order...")
    _, errCreate := orderServiceClient.Create(ctx,
        &order.CreateOrderRequest{
        UserId:    23,
        ProductId: 123,
        Price:     12.3,
    })
    if errCreate != nil {
        log.Printf("Failed to create order. Err: %v", errCreate)
    } else {
        log.Println("Order is created successfully.")
    }
...
```

**The total timeout is three seconds.**

We will get an error here because `OrderServiceClient` has three seconds as a timeout value, and the Order and Product services have at least a four-second delay, which causes a timeout in `OrderServiceClient`. Now that we understand how context is used for the timeout pattern to trigger a failure in the service chain instead of waiting for an unknown period of time, let's look at the retry pattern.

### 6.1.2   Retry pattern

Transient faults occur when a momentary loss of service functionality self-corrects. The retry pattern in gRPC enables us to retry a failed call automatically and thus is perfect for transient faults such as these:

- Instant network failures
- Temporarily unavailable services
- Resource exhaustion of service due to load

gRPC has an interception mechanism that allows you to implement your interceptor and configure the gRPC client to apply the interceptor to all gRPC calls. Using the same strategy, we can execute interceptors on the gRPC server side before the request is passed to actual business logic. gRPC middleware is a good place to define the retry pattern and apply it to all gRPC calls on the client side instead of duplicating retry logic for each type of client call. Thanks to the gRPC ecosystem, a GitHub organization contains notable, community-maintained projects related to gRPC for resiliency. We will use the gRPC retry module (http://mng.bz/XNV9) of go-grpc-middleware (https://github.com/grpc-ecosystem/go-grpc-middleware) to apply retry logic to our gRPC calls.

Assume that the Order service calls the Shipping service, but the Shipping service is unavailable at that time due to very short maintenance. Without a retry mechanism, the Order service will get a failure from the shipping call and mark that order as failed. With a proper retry mechanism, the Order service can retry this call a couple more times and succeed once the Shipping service is back online. We can use the following example if we want to execute five one-second retries once we get either an `Unavailable` or `ResourceExhausted` response code from the Shipping service.

**Listing 6.3  Retry pattern for resiliency**

```
...
imports (
grpc_retry "github.com/grpc-ecosystem/go-grpc-middleware/retry"
"google.golang.org/grpc/codes"
)
...
var opts []grpc.DialOption
    opts = append(opts,
        grpc.WithUnaryInterceptor(grpc_retry.UnaryClientInterceptor(
        grpc_retry.WithCodes(codes.Unavailable, codes.ResourceExhausted),
        grpc_retry.WithMax(5),
        grpc_retry.WithBackoff(grpc_retry.BackoffLinear(time.Second)),
    )))
    opts = append(opts, grpc.WithInsecure())
    conn, err := grpc.Dial("localhost:8080", opts...)
    if err != nil {
        log.Fatalf("Failed to connect shipping service. Err: %v", err)
    }

    defer conn.Close()

    shippingServiceClient := shipping.NewShippingServiceClient(conn)
    log.Println("Creating shipping...")
    _, errCreate := shippingServiceClient.Create(context.Background(),
        &shipping.CreateShippingRequest{
```

Annotations:
- **Enables interceptor for Unary connections** → `grpc.WithUnaryInterceptor(grpc_retry.UnaryClientInterceptor(`
- **Retries only once those codes are returned** → `grpc_retry.WithCodes(codes.Unavailable, codes.ResourceExhausted),`
- **Retries five times at max** → `grpc_retry.WithMax(5),`
- **Uses a one-second timeout for each retry** → `grpc_retry.WithBackoff(grpc_retry.BackoffLinear(time.Second)),`

```
        UserId:  23,
        OrderId: 2344,                                      May return
    })                                          ContextDeadlineExceeded
    if errCreate != nil {
        log.Printf("Failed to create shipping. Err: %v", errCreate)  ◁──┘
    } else {
        log.Println("Shipping is created successfully.")
    }
```

In gRPC, there are two types of interceptor usage, `WithUnaryInterceptor` and `With-StreamingInterceptor` for unary and streaming (http://mng.bz/yQop) connections, respectively. As in listing 6.3, you can use `UnaryClientInterceptor` with or without values; if you don't pass a value, it will use default values for retry, or you can override them by using additional configurations such as `WithCodes`, `WithMax`, or `WithBackoff`. Keep in mind that the gRPC retry configuration is handled via the `grpc_retry` package.

`WithCodes` is used for deciding when to retry, and its default value is the total of the `Unavailable` and `ResourceExhausted` lists. `Unavailable` code is the default since retrying until the service becomes available is beneficial for the client to recover the gRPC call once the dependent service becomes available. In the same way, `ResourceExhausted` is a default because the client might have performed multiple calls that caused the server to apply throttling. For this kind of case, the server will remove throttling, and the client will succeed on the next calls performed by the retry. With these defaults, the retry pattern is applied only if you get `Unavailable` or `ResourceExhausted` from the service call.

The `WithMax` parameter helps to set a maximum limit for retries during interservice communication. If the dependent service becomes available earlier, the client will not retry until the maximum count; it will stop once the client starts to get a response code other than `Unavailable` or `ResourceExhausted`.

`WithBackoff` requires a function to specify back-off functionality between retries. In our example, `BackoffLinear` is used, which means there is a one-second wait time between retries. There are other options, such as `BackoffExponential`, in which the timeout interval on the next retry is multiplied by two, compared to the current timeout interval. Other options are `BackoffLinearWithJitter` and `BackoffExponentialWith-Jitter`, in which the next timeout interval is decided randomly. This randomness reduces the collision of gRPC calls clients make. See http://mng.bz/MB1Q for the details of backoff strategies.

The retry pattern works well for covering transient failures, but if we don't know how long the problem will last, we may end up putting a high load on dependent services with infinite retries. Let's look at a smarter version of the retry pattern that breaks the connection altogether: the circuit breaker pattern.

### 6.1.3 *Circuit breaker pattern*

In the circuit breaker pattern, connections between services are also called circuits, and if the error rate of an interservice communication reaches a threshold value, it opens that circuit, which means the connection between two services is closed intentionally.

After this point, any request to the dependent service will immediately fail due to the open circuit. Of course, this is not a permanent situation; it will be reset after a certain time based on your configuration, and if there is no failure in new requests, the circuit will be closed again. Once the reset timeout is triggered, the state will go into a half-open state, and become closed if there is no other failure. If it continues to get failures, it will go back into an open state (figure 6.3).

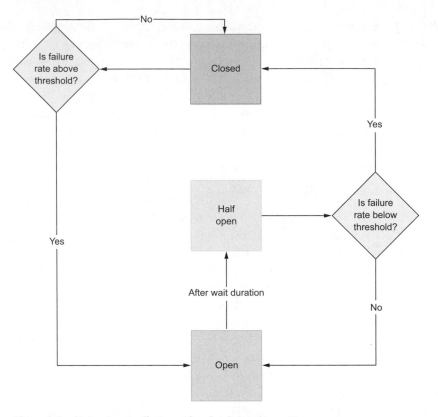

**Figure 6.3   State change diagram of a circuit breaker pattern**

Now that we understand what the circuit breaker pattern, let's look at a Go example to understand production use cases.

Circuit breaker implementations allow your business logic to know the result of your execution and decide the next step in the circuit breaker state machine. You can define several circuit breakers with different configurations and apply them to different parts of your application. In this book, we use a Go circuit breaker. (You can see the source code here: https://github.com/sony/gobreaker.) Before diving deep into the implementation, let's explore the relevant terms in a circuit breaker implementation:

- `MaxRequests` limits the number of requests allowed to pass through a half-open circuit. The difference between an open and half-open circuit is that a half-open one allows certain requests to pass through the circuit based on your configuration, whereas you can't pass through an open request.
- `Interval` mainly defines when the count is cleared while the state is closed. For some use cases, you may not want to clear the interval, even if it has been a long time since you last saw a failure. However, this interval is cleared for most use cases to allow users to make failures within a reasonable time interval.
- `Timeout` decides when to change a circuit breaker state from an open to a half-open state. The advantage of this change is that in an open state, the requests will fail fast, whereas in a half-open state, the circuit breaker allows passing through a half-open circuit by limiting the number of requests.
- `ReadyToTrip` checks the state of the failure threshold after the last failure and decides on whether to open the circuit completely.
- `OnStateChange` is mainly used for tracking state changes while handling business models within a function wrapper.

With this very basic explanation of the configurations of a circuit breaker out of the way, let's design client-server communication using a circuit breaker pattern with the following characteristics:

- The maximum allowed failure (`failed_request_count` / `total_request_count`) ratio is 0.6.
- The `MaxRequests` allowed during the half-open state is 3.
- The timeout value needed for state transition from open to half-open is 4 seconds.
- Print a log statement whenever the state changes.

To implement these requirements, we can simply initialize `*gobreaker.CircuitBreaker` with configurations and wrap a random function to simulate circuit breaker behavior. This random function generates a random number between 10 and 30, and if the generated number is 25, it also returns an error. This error increases the failure count in the circuit breaker, which causes the state to change from closed to open.

#### Listing 6.4 Circuit breaker for simple function

```
package main

import (
    "errors"
    "github.com/sony/gobreaker"
    "log"
    "math/rand"
)

var cb *gobreaker.CircuitBreaker

func main() {
```

Unique
name for
the circuit
breaker

Timeout for
an open to
half-open
transition

```
cb = gobreaker.NewCircuitBreaker(gobreaker.Settings{
    Name:        "demo",
    MaxRequests: 3,      ⟵——— Allowed number of requests for a half-open circuit
    Timeout:     4,
    ReadyToTrip: func(counts gobreaker.Counts) bool {      ⟵
        failureRatio := float64(counts.TotalFailures) /
        ⟹ float64(counts.Requests)
        return failureRatio >= 0.6
    },
    OnStateChange: func(name string, from gobreaker.State, to   ⟵
    ⟹ gobreaker.State) {
        log.Printf("Circuit Breaker: %s, changed from %v, to %v", name,
        ⟹ from, to)
    },
})
cbRes, cbErr := cb.Execute(func() (interface{}, error) {   ⟵
    res, isErr := isError()
    if isErr {
        return nil, errors.New("error")
    }
    return res, nil
})
if cbErr != nil {      ⟵
    log.Fatalf("Circuit breaker error %v", cbErr)
} else {
    log.Printf("Circuit breaker result %v", cbRes)
}
}

func isError() (int, bool) {      ⟵
    min := 10
    max := 30
    result := rand.Intn(max-min) + min
    return result, result != 20
}
```

Decides on
if the circuit
will be open

Executed on each
state change

Wrapped function
to apply a circuit
breaker

**Returns an error once
the circuit is open**

**Random number between
10–30 with error logic**

We wrapped a simple function with circuit breaker logic. Let's apply this logic to a client-server example in which the client tries to create an order periodically, and an exception for some requests is thrown due to an outage in the Order service. For this kind of error case, applying the circuit breaker pattern to client-server interaction is beneficial instead of blindly sending requests.

**Listing 6.5   Client-side circuit breaker**

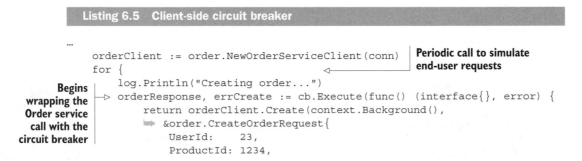

Begins
wrapping the
Order service
call with the
circuit breaker

```
...
orderClient := order.NewOrderServiceClient(conn)    Periodic call to simulate
for {                                        ⟵      end-user requests
    log.Println("Creating order...")
    orderResponse, errCreate := cb.Execute(func() (interface{}, error) {
        return orderClient.Create(context.Background(),
        ⟹ &order.CreateOrderRequest{
            UserId:    23,
            ProductId: 1234,
```

```
                        Price:       3.2,
                    })
            })

        if errCreate != nil {                  ← Error when state changes
            log.Printf("Failed to create order. Err: %v", errCreate)
        } else {
            log.Printf("Order %d is created successfully.",
    orderResponse.(*order.CreateOrderResponse).OrderId)
        }
        time.Sleep(1 * time.Second)            ←
    }                                                 Waits for one second
...                                                   to not heat the CPU
```

**If the circuit is closed, it returns data.** (annotation pointing to `if errCreate != nil { ... } else {`)

**Finishes wrapping** (annotation pointing to `}`)

Suppose you have multiple places like this where you call a dependent service from a consumer service. Would you apply a circuit breaker pattern to all calls by wrapping them? Or would you want some central place to manage the circuit breaker pattern? Let's look at how we can control circuit breaker logic in one place using gRPC interceptors.

Remember, we already used `UnaryClientInterceptor` while handling a retry operation for client-server communication. Now we will implement an interceptor that allows us to pass circuit breaker logic as a parameter to ensure we return `UnaryClientInterceptor`.

---

**Listing 6.6  Circuit breaker interceptor**

```
package middleware

import (
    "context"
    "github.com/sony/gobreaker"
    "google.golang.org/grpc"
)

func CircuitBreakerClientInterceptor(cb *gobreaker.CircuitBreaker)
    grpc.UnaryClientInterceptor {              ←
    return func(                                   A function with a
    ctx context.Context,                           UnaryClientInterceptor type
    method string,
    req, reply interface{},
    cc *grpc.ClientConn,
    invoker grpc.UnaryInvoker,
    opts ...grpc.CallOption,
    ) error {
        _, cbErr := cb.Execute(func() (interface{}, error) {
            err := invoker(ctx, method, req, reply, cc, opts...)
            if err != nil {                                    ←
                return nil, err                          The gRPC call is
            }                                            resumed within a circuit
                                                         breaker wrapper.
            return nil, nil

        })
```

**Circuit breaker wrapper** (annotation pointing to `_, cbErr := cb.Execute(func() (interface{}, error) {`)

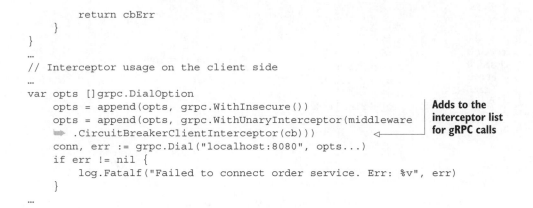

```
            return cbErr
        }
    }
    …
    // Interceptor usage on the client side
    …
    var opts []grpc.DialOption
        opts = append(opts, grpc.WithInsecure())
        opts = append(opts, grpc.WithUnaryInterceptor(middleware
        ➥ .CircuitBreakerClientInterceptor(cb)))
        conn, err := grpc.Dial("localhost:8080", opts...)
        if err != nil {
            log.Fatalf("Failed to connect order service. Err: %v", err)
        }
    …
```

Adds to the interceptor list for gRPC calls

Client interceptors are responsible for modifying/enriching requests before reaching the server side, whereas server interceptors are responsible for applying some logic before using it in server-side business logic (figure 6.4).

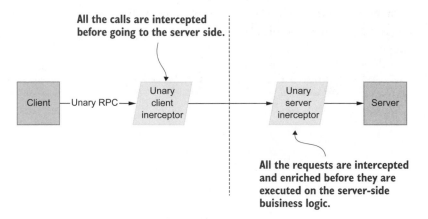

**Figure 6.4   Client- and server-side interceptors**

Now that we know resilient communication patterns in a microservice architecture, let's look at how we can improve resiliency by providing a proper error-handling mechanism to interservice communication.

## 6.2    *Error handling*

Error handling affects the resiliency of interservice communication in a microservices architecture. For a typical client-server communication scenario, the handling response is very trivial, but it becomes complicated once you need to handle errors. Your application must decide what happens next based on the error code in the gRPC response. For example, your application decides whether to retry the request or apply a circuit breaker pattern if you get an error from the server, such as {code: Resource-Exhausted, message: Order Limit Exceeded}. Notice that instead of simply throwing an exception, we can retry later since `Order Limit` will be available soon. Unstructured error messages can also complicate decision making with ambiguity. If any service returns error messages without code, it might be challenging to understand what happened on the server side. Therefore, gRPC provides a status package to handle errors in a more structured way.

### 6.2.1 gRPC error model

gRPC conveniently disambiguates error handling with a reliable error response structure (figure 6.5). In a typical error response, you can see three primary fields: `Code`, `Status`, and `Message`. The `Code` field contains the response code (see all the available codes here: http://mng.bz/a1Vj). `Status` is the human-friendly version of the `Code` field and primarily describes the meaning of `Code` in a couple of words, such as `Bad Request` for `400`. The `Message` field contains a message that explains the error situation in an understandable format. For example, `Email address is invalid` explains to the end user why a registration failed during the `Register gRPC` call. You can also see the `ErrorDetails` section for the error types that contain a list of errors. For example, if a customer submits a register form, you can return multiple error messages under the `ErrorDetails` field explaining which fields are problematic.

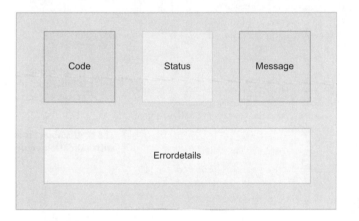

**Figure 6.5   gRPC error model**

Now that we are familiar with the gRPC error model, let's look at how we can implement an Order service endpoint that returns an error response with a detail that the client side correctly handles.

### 6.2.2 gRPC error response

Let's check the requirements for client-server interaction to better understand error-handling logic:

- The client sends a `Create` order request with `product_id`, `user_id`, and `price` parameters.

- The server validates those parameters, generates an error model, and returns it to the client.
- The client converts that response to an error model and determines the validation errors.

**Listing 6.7   Server-client validation**

```
...
import "google.golang.org/grpc/status"

func (s *server) Create(ctx context.Context, in *order.CreateOrderRequest)
    (*order.CreateOrderResponse, error) {
    var validationErrors []*errdetails.BadRequest_FieldViolation
    if in.UserId < 1 {                                              ←
        validationErrors = append(validationErrors,
            &errdetails.BadRequest_FieldViolation{
            Field:       "user_id",
            Description: "user id cannot be less than 1",
        })
    }
    if in.ProductId < 0 {          ←
        validationErrors = append(validationErrors,
            &errdetails.BadRequest_FieldViolation{
            Field:       "product_id",
            Description: "product id cannot be negative",
        })
    }
    if len(validationErrors) > 0 {
        stat := status.New(400, "invalid order request")
        badRequest := &errdetails.BadRequest{}          ←
        badRequest.FieldViolations = validationErrors
        s, _ := stat.WithDetails(badRequest)          ←
        return nil, s.Err()
    }
    return &order.CreateOrderResponse{OrderId: 1243}, nil
}
...
```

**Field violation is added to the error list as a bad request.**

**Validates the user ID and prepares a violation error**

**Validates the product ID**

**Product field validation is added as a bad request item.**

**Error list is added to FieldValidations.**

**A bad request object is initialized under the status object.**

**The status object is augmented with validation errors.**

Now let's look at how we can handle errors on the client side if the server returns a validation error:

```
...
import "google.golang.org/grpc/status"

orderResponse, errCreate := orderClient.Create(context.Background(),
    &order.CreateOrderRequest{
        UserId:    -1,
        ProductId: 0,
        Price:     2,
    })

    if errCreate != nil {
```

The client
converts an
error into an
error model.

```
stat := status.Convert(errCreate)
for _, detail := range stat.Details() {
    switch errType := detail.(type) {        Based on error type,
    case *errdetails.BadRequest:              prints error descriptions
        for _, violation := range errType.GetFieldViolations() {
            log.Printf("The field %s has invalid value. desc: %v",
            ➥ violation.GetField(), violation.GetDescription())
        }
    }
}
} else {
    log.Printf("Order %d is created successfully.",
    ➥ orderResponse.OrderId)
}
...
```

The client side can decide what to do next since it parses the error response and checks fields to understand what is happening with the message. Extended error messages are always beneficial because they may also affect retry and circuit breaker patterns during communication. For example, you can open/close a circuit based on the status code you return from the server side, or retry once you see a specific status code. Now that we better understand gRPC error handling, let's look at securing gRPC communication.

## 6.3 Securing gRPC communication

In this section, we visit the security aspect of the microservices environment. We will skip some topics, such as encrypting TLS certificate passwords, for simplification. In a production environment with many microservices, it is a best practice to delegate certificate generation to a third party, which we will see in detail in chapter 8.

In a microservices environment, services exchange data for different purposes: resource creation, resource aggregation, and so on. The security of this communication is critical and is mostly addressed by encrypting the communication so that nobody can change it when it travels in the network. TLS (Transport Layer Security) helps us provide an encryption protocol for interservice communication. Notice that TLS is the successor of a Secure Sockets Layer (SSL; you probably have heard SSL more often than TLS).

### 6.3.1 TLS handshake

In TLS communication, there is a procedure for securing the communication via public key encryption using a public and private key called a *TLS handshake*. Public key information is stored in a TLS certificate and contains basic information: issuer, expiration date, and so on. In figure 6.6, you can see the minimum required steps for a TLS handshake between the Order and Payment Services:

1  The Order service connects the Payment service.
2  The Payment service shows its certificate to the Order service.

3  The Order service verifies that certificate.

4  The Order service sends data to the Payment service in an encrypted communication channel.

**Figure 6.6   The Order-Payment communication TLS handshake**

As you can see, only the server provides its certificate to let the client verify it. However, there is another version of this handshake in which the client shows its certificate and the server verifies it. This type of handshake is called *mTLS* (mutual TLS), which contains server verification. Figure 6.7 illustrates these steps :

1  The Order service connects to the Payment service.

2  The Payment service shows its certificate to the Order service.

3  The Order service verifies that certificate.

4  The Order service shows its certificate to the Payment service.

5  The Payment service verifies that certificate and allows the Order service to send requests.

6  The Order service sends data to the Payment service in an encrypted communication channel.

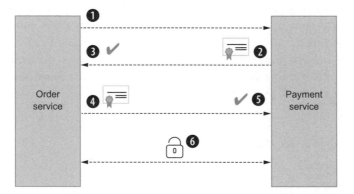

**Figure 6.7   Order-Payment service mTLS communication**

With mTLS, you simply secure the connection between the Order service and the Payment service in both directions. Whenever there is a connection to those services, the identity will be extracted, and both sides will know the owner of a specific call. This approach is beneficial for organizations that use a zero-trust approach for their network security. Next, let's prepare a certificate for the Go microservices example.

### 6.3.2 Certificate generation

We will use the OpenSSL (https://www.openssl.org/source/) tool to generate self-signed certificates. A certificate authority (CA) is responsible for storing, signing, and issuing digital certificates. This means we will first generate a private key and a self-signed certificate for the certificate authority:

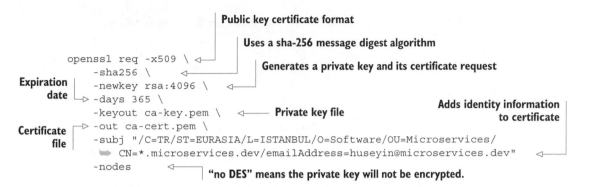

We will not encrypt the private key of the certificate, but in upcoming chapters, we will automate certificate generation for production use cases with the private key encrypted.

The `-subj` parameter contains identity information about the certificate:

- `/C` is used for country.
- `/ST` is the state information.
- `/L` states city information.
- `/O` means organization.
- `/OU` is for the organization unit to explain which department.
- `/CN` is used for the domain name, the short version of common name.
- `/emailAddress` is used for an email address to contact the certificate owner.

You can verify the generated self-certificate for the CA with the following command:

```
openssl x509 -in ca-cert.pem -noout -text
```

Once you verify it, we can proceed with the private key and certificate signing request:

Then we will use CA's private key to sign the request:

```
openssl x509 \
    -req -in server-req.pem \          ⟵——— Passes the sign request
    -days 60 \
    -CA ca-cert.pem \
    -CAkey ca-key.pem \           Generates the next serial
    -CAcreateserial \          ⟵——— number for the certificate
    -out server-cert.pem \
    -extfile server-ext.cnf \     ⟵——— Additional configs for the certificate
    -sha256
```

**CA's certificate** and **CA's private key** labels point to `-CA ca-cert.pem` and `-CAkey ca-key.pem` respectively.

An example configuration for ext file option is as follows:

```
subjectAltName=DNS:*.microservices.dev,DNS:*.microservices.dev,IP:0.0.0.0
```

Now you can verify the server's self-signed certificate:

```
openssl x509 -in server-cert.pem -noout -text
```

For mTLS communication, we need to generate a certificate signing request for the client side, so let's generate a private key and this self-signed certificate:

```
openssl req \
    -newkey rsa:4096 \
    -keyout client-key.pem \
    -out client-req.pem \
    -subj "/C=TR/ST=EURASIA/L=Istanbul/O=Microservices/OU=OrderService/
    ➥ CN=*.microservices.dev/emailAddress=huseyin@microservices.dev" \
    -nodes \
    -sha256
```

Now, let's sign it using the CA's private key:

```
openssl x509 \
    -req -in client-req.pem \
    -sha256 \
    -days 60 \
    -CA ca.crt \
    -CAkey ca.key \
    -CAcreateserial \
    -out client.crt \
    -extfile client-ext.cnf
```

Finally, you can verify the client certificate with the following command:

```
openssl x509 -in client-cert.pem -noout -text
```

Now the server certificate can be used on the server side, which is the Payment service, in our case. Let's look at how we can integrate those certificates into Payment and Order services.

### 6.3.3 gRPC TLS credentials

Adding certificate information to a server implementation is twofold: implement logic to load credentials and create a `TransportCredentials` (http://mng.bz/gBAe) instance; then use this function within the interceptor to handle credentials verification out of the box for each request. This means the following steps are applied (figure 6.8):

1 The client sends a gRPC call to the server.
2 The server presents its shared certificate with its public key.
3 The client validates this certificate on a CA. For now, the CA cert contains client and server shared certificates.
4 After client validation, the client presents its shared certificate with its public key to the server.
5 The server validates the shared certificate on the CA.
6 After successful verification, the client receives a response from the gRPC call.

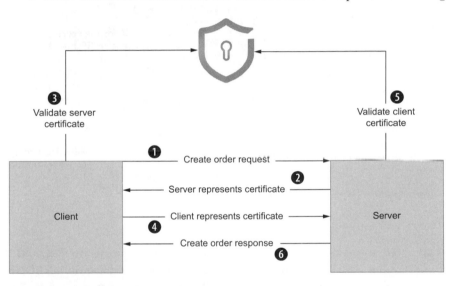

**Figure 6.8  gRPC communication with mTLS**

If we wanted to implement this flow on the client and server side, we could use already generated shared certificates for both the server and client side. Since the CA signs the certificate, those shared certificates (`client.crt`, `server.crt`) are already in `ca.crt`. For development purposes, we will generate a `cert` pool in the server and client and append client and server certificates there. Finally, we will put TLS configuration inside gRPC server options.

**Listing 6.8   gRPC TLS configuration**

```
...
func getTlsCredentials() (credentials.TransportCredentials, error) {
    serverCert, serverCertErr := tls.LoadX509KeyPair("cert/server.crt",
        "cert/server.key")
    // handle serverCertErr
    certPool := x509.NewCertPool()
    caCert, caCertErr := ioutil.ReadFile("cert/ca.crt")
    // handle caCertErr
    if ok := certPool.AppendCertsFromPEM(caCert); !ok {
        return nil, errors.New("failed to append the CA certs")
    }

    return credentials.NewTLS(
        &tls.Config{
            ClientAuth:   tls.RequireAnyClientCert,
            Certificates: []tls.Certificate{serverCert},
            ClientCAs:    certPool,
        }), nil
}
...
func main() {

    listener, err := net.Listen("tcp", fmt.Sprintf(":%d", 8080))
    // handle err
    tlsCredentials, tlsCredentialsErr := getTlsCredentials()
    // handle tlsCredentialsErr
    var opts []grpc.ServerOption
    opts = append(opts, grpc.Creds(tlsCredentials))

    grpcServer := grpc.NewServer(opts...)
    ...
}
```

Annotations:
- **Certificate pool for CA check** → `certPool := x509.NewCertPool()`
- **Adds ca.crt to pool** → `if ok := certPool.AppendCertsFromPEM(caCert); !ok {`
- **Load server certificate** → `"cert/server.key")`
- **Client authentication type** → `ClientAuth:   tls.RequireAnyClientCert,`
- **Provides server certificate** → `Certificates: []tls.Certificate{serverCert},`
- **Roots the CA for the server to verify client certificates** → `ClientCAs:    certPool,`
- **Adds TLS configuration to server options** → `opts = append(opts, grpc.Creds(tlsCredentials))`

In listing 6.8, transport credentials are created from the certificate files, and the newly created credentials object is passed to the gRPC server initialization. This also means that when a client wants to connect this gRPC server, it must provide a client certificate to its gRPC client connections.

Now that the server side has TLS configuration enabled, let's look at how we can configure the client side to let the client and server exchange their certificates and then establish secure communication:

```
func getTlsCredentials() (credentials.TransportCredentials, error) {
    clientCert, clientCertErr := tls.LoadX509KeyPair("cert/client.crt",
        "cert/client.key")
    // handle clientCertErr

    certPool := x509.NewCertPool()
    caCert, caCertErr := ioutil.ReadFile("cert/ca.crt")
    // handle caCertErr
```

Annotations:
- **Loads client certificate** → `"cert/client.key")`
- **Certificate pool for CA check** → `certPool := x509.NewCertPool()`

```
                    if ok := certPool.AppendCertsFromPEM(caCert); !ok {
                        return nil, errors.New("failed to append CA cert.")
                    }
```
**Adds the CA to the certificate pool**

**Provides the client certificate**
```
    return credentials.NewTLS(&tls.Config{
        ServerName:    "*.microservices.dev",
        Certificates: []tls.Certificate{clientCert},
        RootCAs:       certPool,
    }), nil
}
...
func main() {
    tlsCredentials, tlsCredentialsErr := getTlsCredentials()
    // handle tlsCredentialsErr
    var opts []grpc.DialOption

    opts = append(opts, grpc.WithTransportCredentials(tlsCredentials))
    conn, err := grpc.Dial("localhost:8080", opts...)
    // handle err
}
...
```
**Server name used during certificate generation**

**Roots the CA for the client to verify the server certificate**

**Adds TLS configuration to gRPC dial options**

This implementation is useful for local development, but in a production environment, it is best practice to delegate certificate management to a third party, which we will see in detail in chapter 8 when we deploy microservices to a Kubernetes environment.

## Summary

- In a typical microservices architecture, it is normal for one service to depend on one or more other services. If one of the dependent services is down, it will affect the availability of the entire microservice application. We use resiliency patterns such as retry, timeout, and circuit breaker to prevent these situations.

- Once the dependent service is down, we can use the retry strategy on the consumer side to make gRPC communication eventually succeed.

- Retry logic can be triggered for certain status codes, such as `Unavailable` or `ResourceExhausted`, instead of blindly retrying on each failure. For example, it is not wise to retry a request if you received a validation exception because it shows that you sent an invalid payload; you should fix it to make it succeed.

- Using retry logic blocks the actual gRPC call since you have to wait for dependent service. It is hard to detect recovery time for a dependent service, which can create long wait times for retries. To prevent this situation, we use context timeout and deadline to put a time limit on blocking the actual execution.

- In the retry mechanism, you can redo an operation for specific time intervals, but this can also put an extra load on the dependent service since it has to retry all the time, even if the dependent service is not ready. To solve this problem, we use a circuit breaker to open a circuit once we reach the failure limit, retry the request after some time, and finally close the circuit once the dependent service is back online.

- Error handling is important in interservice communication because the next step is decided from error codes or messages in the gRPC response. We use a status package to return customized errors from a service, and we can convert them on the client side once needed.
- Resiliency is important not only in communication patterns, but also in zero-trust environments, in which we use TLS-enabled communications, as the server and client verify their certificates during gRPC communications. This is also called mutual TLS.

# Testing microservices

7

**This chapter covers**

- Understanding the motivation behind testing
- Test strategies (e.g., unit testing, integration testing, and end-to-end testing)
- Test containers' usage in test automation
- Calculating and viewing the test coverage for test suites
- Understanding test pyramids

Microservice architecture encourages you to write minimal services that can be easily tested as a unit. For example, while testing the Order service, the only context you need to focus on is Order. To test the Order service, you have two high-level alternatives: manual testing and automated testing.

With manual testing, you must run actual and dependent services to test the entire flow. This can be a time-consuming operation compared to testing backed by a machine. This inefficient testing methodology will also slow down your software delivery. However, with automated testing, you can get fast feedback from your implementation because you don't need to wait until you finish and test the entire system.

We will look at different testing strategies in this chapter, but first let's look at the relations between them and their possible advantages and disadvantages.

> **About code examples in this chapter**
>
> In chapter 4, we started coding our services, and in this chapter, we depend on what we implemented in chapter 4 and chapter 5 and continue to extend the code. Even though you will see step-by-step explanations of different testing strategies, you can always check the completed version here: https://github.com/huseyinbabal/microservices.

## 7.1  Testing pyramid

The testing pyramid organizes software tests into three categories based on their context and provides insight into the percentage of tests for each category:

- *Unit tests*—Type of software test in which specific units of software are tested
- *Integration tests*—Type of software test in which the integration of multiple modules is tested
- *End-to-end tests*—Type of software test in which the entire behavior of the application is tested

The unit test category is at the bottom of the pyramid, the integration test is in the middle, and the end-to-end test is at the top (figure 7.1).

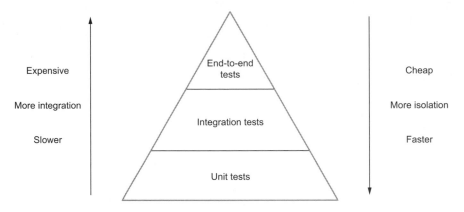

**Figure 7.1   Testing pyramid**

As you can see, in a typical application, the percentage of unit tests is greater than that for integration tests, which is greater than the percentage for end-to-end tests. There are possible reasons/outputs for that percentage; let's analyze them individually.

Unit tests are designed to test one component at a time, with maximum isolation. While testing a component (SUT), you should mock the other dependencies. Isolation levels get lower once you move up on the pyramid because you start to involve more components in the test suite that might break the isolation.

In a unit test, you probably have a test runner, enough to test the core features and mock the dependencies. Once you move to the integration test, you need third-party tools to maintain dependencies, such as having test containers for a DB connection.

Once you start to use third parties, test execution will slow down to wait for all the dependent components.

Going from a unit test to an end-to-end test has cost increases because more components mean more resource consumption, and thus more money. The unit test has the greatest percentage of the pyramid because it is fast and cheap. In the same way, the end-to-end test has the lowest percentage of the pyramid because it is expensive and slow to run. This does not mean you need to write a unit test but not an end-to-end test. It does mean you should arrange the percentage of test types as stated in the test pyramid. Now that we can see the relations between testing strategies, let's look at how those strategies are used to verify the microservice application behavior.

## 7.2    Testing with a unit test

Automated testing gives faster feedback, and thus saves on time and cost. Unit tests are good for verifying one basic operation unit at a time, but is that enough to verify your implementation? We will see different testing strategies, such as integration and end-to-end tests, but let's look at a SUT first.

### 7.2.1    System under test

The SUT test contains inputs, execution conditions, and expected results to verify its behavior within a codebase. A SUT means a software element is being tested. Based on your testing strategy, a SUT can be a class or an entire application. This test is important if you are testing a specific layer in hexagonal architecture because you need to know what to test in that layer. It becomes a test suite if you group related tests to verify the behavior of a SUT. In figure 7.2, one happy path and three edge case tests form a test suite to verify different kinds of SUT behavior.

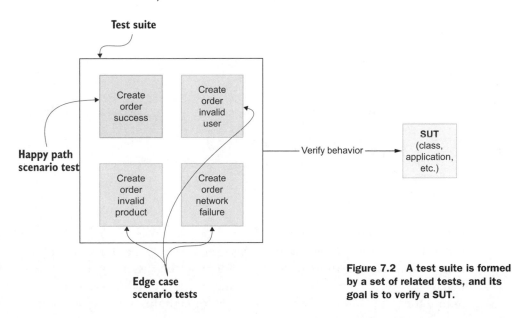

Figure 7.2   A test suite is formed by a set of related tests, and its goal is to verify a SUT.

### 7.2.2   *Test workflow*

Before diving into the internals of testing frameworks and writing actual Go code, let's start with the phases of an automated test:

1 *Setup*—In this phase, we prepare the dependencies of a SUT and initialize a SUT with them. This can also involve initializing third-party dependencies, such as a MySQL database.
2 *Invoke the SUT*—If we are testing a class, in this phase, we might call a function from that class.
3 *Verify*—Verify the actual result with the expected result by using assertions.
4 *Teardown*—Clean up resources that are no longer needed. For example, we could destroy the MySQL database once we are done with it.

You may not need setup and teardown phases for some tests, which contain very simple logic. For example, to test the following `Fibonacci` behavior from the `math` class, you can call the SUT, `Fibonacci()`, and compare the actual result with the expected result:

```go
// math.go
package math

func Fibonacci(n int) int {    ◁——— Returns a value at the nth position
    if n <= 1 {
        return n
    }
    return Fibonacci(n-1) + Fibonacci(n-2)
}
```

To implement test cases for the `Fibonacci` function, you can create another file with the _test.go suffix and execute it via the `go test` command:

```go
// math_test.go
package math

import (
    "testing"

    "github.com/stretchr/testify/assert"    ◁——— External assertion library
)

func TestFibonacci(t *testing.T) {
    actual := Fibonacci(3)
    expected := 2
    assert.Equal(t, actual, expected)
}
```

Go has built-in libraries for testing, but you may want to use other third-party libraries for better test suite management. In this example, we use a third-party library, `testify` (https://github.com/stretchr/testify), a unit testing assertion library, to verify the behavior of SUTs. Since the `Fibonacci` function does not depend on other systems, we ignore the setup and teardown phases, even though this is not typical in microservices architecture. For example, the Order service depends on a MySQL database, and to test Order features, you need to prepare dependent systems with one of the following:

- Spin up the database via test containers and provide credentials of a created database instance to the Order service to be able to run it and execute tests against it.
- Mock database-related calls and focus on the Order service.

Since preparing real dependencies would be inefficient because it will slow down the testing process, in this case it's better to use mocking to get fast feedback.

### 7.2.3   *Working with mocks*

Mocking in a test aims to isolate dependent systems' internals and focus only on a SUT to not only have minimal setup for your test, but to also control the behavior of the dependent system based on your needs. Let's say that the Order service depends on the Payment service and Order database, and you want to test one of the scenarios for the `PlaceOrder` functionality in the Order service. If you want to control the behavior of the Order database and Payment service operations, you can mock the Order database and Payment service and then simulate the method calls (figure 7.3).

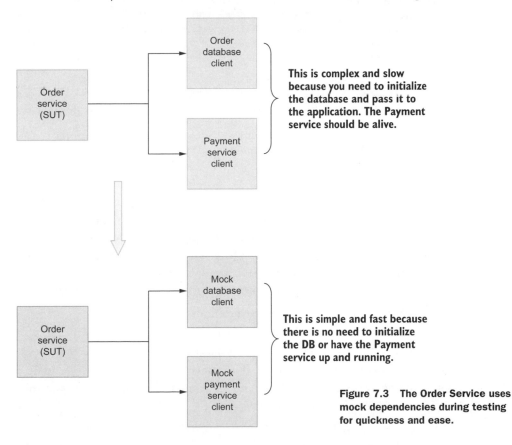

**Figure 7.3   The Order Service uses mock dependencies during testing for quickness and ease.**

Whatever you are trying to mock should be an interface. Since we are using hexagonal architecture, and ports in that architecture are interfaces, we can quickly provide a mock without changing the real implementation. Because we already have `PaymentPort` and `DBPort`, let's look at how we can mock them using a mock library (https://pkg .go.dev/github.com/stretchr/testify/mock).

### 7.2.4   *Implementing a mock*

Here is the `PlaceOrder` implementation from the Order service:

```
type Application struct {
    db      ports.DBPort
    payment ports.PaymentPort
}
…
func (a *Application) PlaceOrder(order domain.Order) (domain.Order, error) {
    err := a.db.Save(&order)
    if err != nil {
        return domain.Order{}, err
    }
    paymentErr := a.payment.Charge(&order)
    if paymentErr != nil {
        st, _ := status.FromError(paymentErr)
        fieldErr := &errdetails.BadRequest_FieldViolation{
            Field:       "payment",
            Description: st.Message(),
        }
        badReq := &errdetails.BadRequest{}
        badReq.FieldViolations = append(badReq.FieldViolations, fieldErr)
        orderStatus := status.New(codes.InvalidArgument, "order creation
➥ failed")
        statusWithDetails, _ := orderStatus.WithDetails(badReq)
        return domain.Order{}, statusWithDetails.Err()
    }
    return order, nil
}
```

In the `Application struct`, we can see there are two dependencies we can mock, and in the `PlaceOrder` function, there is a `db` call and a `payment` service call. We also have error cases for both `db` and `payment` service calls. If we properly mock `payment`- and `db`-related calls, we can easily control the behavior to test branches in the `PlaceOrder` function.

We can use the following steps to create a mock for any interface:

1  Create a mock struct for the payment interface.
2  Embed `mock.Mock` as a field to this struct.
3  Create a receiver function for the `Charge` method.
4  Create a mock struct for the DB interface.
5  Create a receiver function for the `Save` and `Get` functions that have the same signature as stated in a real interface.

```
type mockedPayment struct {
    mock.Mock                      ◁─── Embeds to track the activity of the payment
}

func (p *mockedPayment) Charge(order *domain.Order) error {
    args := p.Called(order)        ◁───┐
    return args.Error(0)   ◁───────────┤   Tracks the function call with arguments
}                                       │
                                        └── Tracks the function return values
type mockedDb struct {
    mock.Mock
}

func (d *mockedDb) Save(order *domain.Order) error {
    args := d.Called(order)
    return args.Error(0)
}

func (d *mockedDb) Get(id string) (domain.Order, error) {
    args := d.Called(id)
    return args.Get(0).(domain.Order), args.Error(1)
}
```

Called() is a method on the mock object we can call directly because it is an anonymous property. (You can see the internals of this usage here: http://mng.bz/5wOq.) Now that we have mock behaviors of the Payment service, let's add a simple test to verify PlaceOrder behavior on the Order service.

To simplify the test, let's say that DB- and payment-related calls don't return an error. In this case, we can verify that application.PlaceOrder does not return an error using an assert library:

```
func Test_Should_Place_Order(t *testing.T) {
    payment := new(mockedPayment)
    db := new(mockedDb)                                     There is no error on
    payment.On("Charge", mock.Anything).Return(nil) ◁──┘    payment.Charge.
    db.On("Save", mock.Anything).Return(nil)   ◁────┐
                                                     └── There is no error on db.Save.
    application := NewApplication(db, payment)
    _, err := application.PlaceOrder(domain.Order{
        CustomerID: 123,
        OrderItems: []domain.OrderItem{
            {
                ProductCode: "camera",
                UnitPrice:   12.3,
                Quantity:    3,
            },
        },
        CreatedAt: 0,
    })
    assert.Nil(t, err)   ◁─── err is null in this case.

}
```

We just wrote a unit test for the happy path scenario, but what happens if there is a problem on the db.Save() method? Let's try to mock an error case to see the behavior change on PlaceOrder:

1 db.Save() method returns an error with some message.

2 Since this happens inside the PlaceOrder() function, we need to verify that the return value contains the error message from db.Save().

To test behavior, implement the following test:

```
func Test_Should_Return_Error_When_Db_Persistence_Fail(t *testing.T) {
    payment := new(mockedPayment)
    db := new(mockedDb)
    payment.On("Charge", mock.Anything).Return(nil)
    db.On("Save", mock.Anything).Return(errors.New("connection error"))    ◁─┐  db.Save() returns a
                                                                               connection error.
    application := NewApplication(db, payment)
    _, err := application.PlaceOrder(domain.Order{
        CustomerID: 123,
        OrderItems: []domain.OrderItem{
            {
                ProductCode: "phone",
                UnitPrice:   14.7,
                Quantity:    1,
            },
        },
        CreatedAt: 0,
    })                                                          application.PlaceOrder() should
    assert.EqualError(t, err, "connection error")   ◁─┐  contain a connection error.
}
```

There could be an error on the payment.Charge() call, and solving this would be a bit complex because it contains a validation error message. Since the message comes from the Payment service, we get only the fields we need and return them to the end user. Let's write a unit test for that flow:

```
func Test_Should_Return_Error_When_Payment_Fail(t *testing.T) {
    payment := new(mockedPayment)
    db := new(mockedDb)
    payment.On("Charge", mock.Anything).Return(errors.New("insufficient
    ➥ balance"))                                        ◁─┐  payment.Charge() fails.
    db.On("Save", mock.Anything).Return(nil)

    application := NewApplication(db, payment)
    _, err := application.PlaceOrder(domain.Order{
        CustomerID: 123,
        OrderItems: []domain.OrderItem{
            {
                ProductCode: "bag",
                UnitPrice:   2.5,
                Quantity:    6,
            },
```

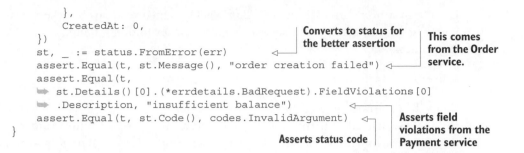

```
        },
        CreatedAt: 0,
    })
    st, _ := status.FromError(err)
    assert.Equal(t, st.Message(), "order creation failed")
    assert.Equal(t,
    ⇒   st.Details()[0].(*errdetails.BadRequest).FieldViolations[0]
    ⇒   .Description, "insufficient balance")
    assert.Equal(t, st.Code(), codes.InvalidArgument)
}
```

Converts to status for the better assertion

This comes from the Order service.

Asserts field violations from the Payment service

Asserts status code

In this unit test, we expect to see an error after calling PlaceOrder and assert the error message and each validation error. To run tests, you can simply execute the following command:

```
go test ./..
```

If you want to see the coverage report in your test results, simply use the following test command:

```
go test ./... -cover -coverprofile=coverage.out
```

With -cover parameter, Go generates the coverage, and a report is written to the file coverage.out with a -coverprofile param. You can see the report in the execution output, as shown in figure 7.4.

Package coverages

Package-level tests passed

Figure 7.4    The output of test execution with coverage

It seems straightforward to create mocks and control the behavior to test a SUT, but what if you have many interfaces in your project? In the next section, we will see how to generate these mocks automatically with simple automation.

### 7.2.5    Automatic mock generation

Hexagonal architecture encourages defining your ports as an interface, then implementing the adapters afterward. It is easy to mock interfaces because mocking libraries need exposed functions of an API. If there are lots of interfaces in your project to mock, you can use mockery (https://github.com/vektra/mockery). There are several options with mockery, and in this book, we will use a mockery executable that can be installed via homebrew if you are using macOS. Once you have mockery available in your system, navigate to your service (e.g., the order folder), then execute the following command/:

```
mockery --all --keeptree
```

You will see autogenerated files, such as *_mock.go, for each interface that contains the mocks. Instead of trying to mock method arguments and return values, mockery does that for us, and we can use those mocks in our unit tests. When they are needed, we can re-create mocks whenever we update an interface or introduce a new one. The flow is the same after generating mocks so that you can control their behavior and test a SUT. Now that we understand how to test individual system modules with unit testing methodology, let's look at how to test the interaction between two modules to verify behavior.

## 7.3    *Integration testing*

In integration testing, we aim to test different modules together to verify they work as expected. For example, we have a DB adapter, and we can test if this adapter works well with a running MySQL database. You may ask, "Why do we want to access a real database?" Because we want to verify our codebase still works in case of a change in code or a version change on the DB side. This section will use Testcontainers (https://www.testcontainers.org/) to spin up a MySQL instance and pass the Testcontainers' URL to a DB adapter. Let's look at how to structure our test suite and initialize a MySQL instance using Testcontainers.

### 7.3.1    *Test suite preparation*

Test suite libraries help you prepare before and after tests and allow you to run your tests with those test preparations. In this book, we use suite (https://github.com/stretchr/testify/tree/master/suite), which comes from testify. You may want to act on the following cases in a test suite:

- *Before each test*—You may want to create a mock before each test instead of manually defining that mock on each test function. We can run an action before each test by adding a method named `TestSetupTest` to our test suite.
- *After each test*—Let's say you interact with files and folders on each test and want to delete them to have a new state on the next test. We can activate such an action by implementing `TestTearDownSuite`.
- *Before all the tests*—We prepare resources for all tests to use because they use a shared resource. For example, we can initialize a database via Testcontainers before running the tests. This action can be activated by implementing `TestSetupSuite`.
- *After all the tests*—Let's say you initialized your DB instance and want to destroy it right after you finish all the tests. We can trigger this action by adding a method named `TestTearDownSuite`.

The flow diagram of test execution is shown in figure 7.5.

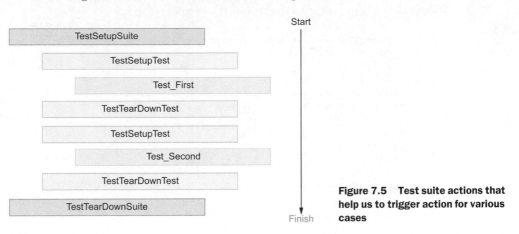

Figure 7.5 **Test suite actions that help us to trigger action for various cases**

To create a test suite, we simply create a struct and embed `suite.Suite` inside it. Let's look at how we can create our test suite to prepare the MySQL test container and use it to test the DB adapter.

### 7.3.2 *Working with Testcontainers*

To use Testcontainers with Go, first, we add the `testcontainers-go` dependency to the Order service project; then use it in our tests to pull and run the MySQL container:

```
go get github.com/testcontainers/testcontainers-go
```

This will add the latest `testcontainers-go` dependency to the Order service project. In a typical Testcontainer setup, you can see the following events:

- A background context
- A container request with an image, exposed ports, and a liveness probe statement that the `Testcontainers` library can use to check whether the running container is ready to accept connections
- Once the container is up and running, a connection URL to use in our tests

Now you can navigate to the order/internal/adapters folder and create a file named db_integration_test.go. The following struct should be added to the test file to define our test suite context:

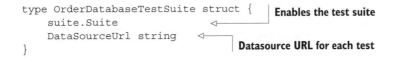

```
type OrderDatabaseTestSuite struct {          Enables the test suite
    suite.Suite
    DataSourceUrl string
}
                                              Datasource URL for each test
```

Now we are ready to add Testcontainers to initialize a MySQL instance in the Docker container in the `TestSetupSuite` function, with the receiver type `OrderDatabaseTestSuite`.

This will create a MySQL container, verify it is up and running, then get the available endpoint URL and pass it to the test suite context:

```
func (o *OrderDatabaseTestSuite) SetupSuite() {          ⟵─┐ Suite setup with
    ctx := context.Background()                              receiver function
    port := "3306/tcp"
    dbURL := func(port nat.Port) string {
        return fmt.Sprintf("root:s3cr3t@tcp(localhost:%s)/
        ➥ orders?charset=utf8mb4&parseTime=True&loc=Local",
        ➥ port.Port())
    }
    req := testcontainers.ContainerRequest{
        Image:       "docker.io/mysql:8.0.30",
        ExposedPorts: []string{port},
        Env: map[string]string{
            "MYSQL_ROOT_PASSWORD": "s3cr3t",
            "MYSQL_DATABASE":      "orders",
        },
        WaitingFor: wait.ForSQL(nat.Port(port), "mysql",    Verifies DB with the
        ➥ dbURL).Timeout(time.Second * 30),      ⟵─┘     SELECT 1 query
    }
    mysqlContainer, err := testcontainers.GenericContainer(ctx,
    ➥ testcontainers.GenericContainerRequest{
        ContainerRequest: req,
        Started:          true,
    })
    if err != nil {
        log.Fatal("Failed to start Mysql.", err)
    }
    endpoint, _ := mysqlContainer.Endpoint(ctx, "")
    o.DataSourceUrl =
    ➥ fmt.Sprintf("root:s3cr3t@tcp(%s)/
    ➥ orders?charset=utf8mb4&parseTime=True&loc=Local", endpoint)   ⟵─
}
```

Annotations (left margin): **Used for a health check in the WaitFor field** — points to dbURL. **Sets DataSourceUrl to be used on each test** — points to the final Sprintf.

A security note here: we have used a root user in our tests, but it is good practice to use a nonroot user for accessing databases. Let's implement a test for verifying DB adapter save functionality and see if MySQL is correctly initialized, then assert there is no error in the test after saving. These tests contain a receiver with the type OrderDatabaseTestSuite so that we have direct access to asserting functions. Now we can append db.Save() testing to the db_integrateion_test.go file:

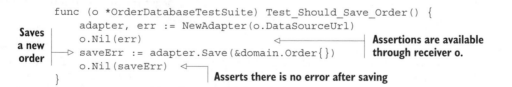

```
func (o *OrderDatabaseTestSuite) Test_Should_Save_Order() {
    adapter, err := NewAdapter(o.DataSourceUrl)
    o.Nil(err)                    ⟵──────────────── Assertions are available
    saveErr := adapter.Save(&domain.Order{})          through receiver o.
    o.Nil(saveErr)  ⟵──┐
}                       Asserts there is no error after saving
```

*Saves a new order*

According to this test, there shouldn't be an error after order information is saved to the database. Let's add one more test for the db.Get() function verification; then we will see how to execute all tests in one suite. Create a sample order and save it to the database, then get it to verify if the returned order contains the same `customerID` we provided the initial order:

```
func (o *OrderDatabaseTestSuite) Test_Should_Get_Order() {
    adapter, _ := NewAdapter(o.DataSourceUrl)
    order := domain.NewOrder(2, []domain.OrderItem{    ◁——— Example order
        {
            ProductCode: "CAM",
            Quantity:    5,
            UnitPrice:   1.32,
        },
    })
    adapter.Save(&order)
    ord, _ := adapter.Get(order.ID)    ◁——— Retrieves the order by its ID
    o.Equal(int64(2), ord.CustomerID)    ◁———
}                                             Equal is accessible via the receiver.
```

Now that we have added all the tests, let's add another function responsible for running them, `suite.Run(..)`, with the argument `OrderDatabaseTestSuite`, which causes all the tests that contain a receiver with this type to run. We can append the following function to our test file as a final step:

```
func TestOrderDatabaseTestSuite(t *testing.T) {     Runs all tests with the
    suite.Run(t, new(OrderDatabaseTestSuite))     ◁——— OrderDatabaseTestSuite receiver
}
```

Now you can navigate to internal/adapters/db and execute the following to run all the tests inside the suite:

```
go test ./...
```

This execution will spin up a test container for MySQL, and the tests will run against that database. This verifies that the DB adapter works well with a real MySQL database. We call it an integration test because we verify that the two modules work together. What if we want to test all the components together? Let's look at how we can verify our application works well with all its dependencies.

## 7.4 End-to-end tests

We addressed testing one component with unit tests and integration tests to check consistency between two components, but to say our product is working, we need more than that. Here, we will do an end-to-end test by running the stack that contains the minimum set of required services and verifying a certain flow against this stack. To accomplish this goal, we will run MySQL database, Payment service, and Order service and use the testing techniques we used for previous sections with an order client to test a create order flow. We will create an order and get order details to assert each response field in that suite. Let's look at high-level information about that setup and dive deep into each section.

### 7.4.1   Specifications

Here are the end-to-end test specifications we will use for our tests:

- Good news if you already have some experience with Docker (https://www.docker .com/): we will use Docker Compose (https://docs.docker.com/compose/) to build our stack, which helps you to define and run your application stack with multiple containers. We will simply create a YAML file and define our services there.
- We will use the suite package again to run our stack via test containers in the SetupSuite phase and destroy that in the TearDownSuite phase.
- We will implement one test case about the create order flow.
- To run our services as a Docker container, we need Dockerfile definitions for each service. We will see new terms for building new Docker images while running test containers in this context.
- We will use mysql:8 for the database layer in our stack, and we will mount an SQL file to this container to create a payments and an orders database in advance.

Based on these specifications, our test diagram will look like figure 7.6.

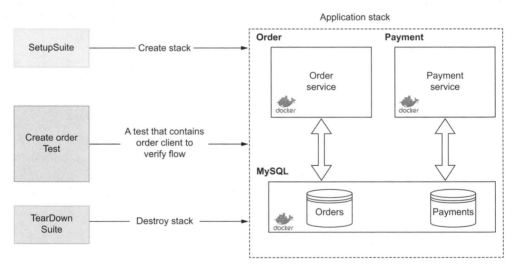

**Figure 7.6   Application stack that test suite runs against**

Now that we see the big picture, let's look at what a Docker Compose YAML files looks like.

### 7.4.2   Understanding Docker Compose service definitions

Docker Compose lets you define service definitions in a YAML file, which contains two major sections: version and services. The version section helps the Docker Compose

CLI understand the YAML file's data structure. The services section defines service dependencies, requirements, and corresponding properties, as follows:

- `build`—This field states the path of the Dockerfile to use during the stack build.
- `environment`—With this field, we can define our environment variables, such as application port. This field accepts a list with key-value pairs.
- `depends_on`—Sometimes, you may need a prerequisite service for your service. To accomplish that, you can use the `depends_on` field. A service that has `depends_on` will not be built until the services defined under this field are ready.
- `ports`—This field contains a port list for a specific service to be accessed from outside.
- `healthcheck`—By default, a service is marked ready once the container is started in a stack. However, the application inside this service may not accept the connection. For this reason, you may need to define a health check condition using this field.
- `volumes`—This field mounts a local resource to the container so that your local resource will be available inside the container. We will use this to mount an SQL file to the `mysql` container so that it will process it at startup.

We will use these fields in this book, but if you are interested in other fields, you can refer to https://docs.docker.com/compose/. Now that we have insight into Docker Compose service fields, let's look at how to structure our end-to-end test.

### 7.4.3 End-to-end test folder structure

To add a separate module to run our end-to-end tests, go to the root folder of our project and create a folder with the name e2e. You can navigate to that folder and initialize a module via the following command:

```
go mod init github.com/huseyinbabal/microservices/e2e
```

Do not forget to replace the username and repository in the go.mod file based on your needs. To store our docker-compose.yml and DB migration files, create a resources folder under the e2e folder. Once you add the docker-compose.yml file to the resources folder, we can proceed with the initial service definitions that contain the database layer. Notice that we just created a separate module dedicated to end-to-end tests that contains a Docker Compose file to define the required service layers for our tests. Let's start with the database layer used by our microservices.

### 7.4.4 Database layer

In this layer, we provide a Docker image, mysql:8.0.30, and a password for the root user. We also have an SQL file mounted to this service. As a health check mechanism, we simply ping the MySQL server, which will be retried 20 times maximum, with a 5-second difference on each retry. If the command result provided in the test field returns true, this service will be marked as ready. You can append the following YAML definition to the docker-compose.yml file:

```
version: "3.9"
services:              Service name as a key
  mysql:      ◄──────
    image: "mysql:8.0.30"
    environment:
      MYSQL_ROOT_PASSWORD: "s3cr3t"                      The SQL file
    volumes:                                             contains DB
      - "./init.sql:/docker-entrypoint-initdb.d/init.sql"  ◄──  creations.
    healthcheck:
      test: ["CMD", "mysqladmin" ,"ping", "-h", "localhost", "-uroot", "-
      ➥ ps3cr3t"]
      interval: 5s
      timeout: 5s
      retries: 20
```

You can create an init.sql file and append the following SQL script to prepare our databases when the MySQL container starts:

```
CREATE DATABASE IF NOT EXISTS payments;
CREATE DATABASE IF NOT EXISTS orders;
```

The following command will provision a MySQL container with the `payments` and `orders` database:

```
cd resources && docker-compose up
```

This command will provision a database container, and before accepting a new connection, it will create two databases and the test section will start to work. Now that we know how to create the database container, let's look at the Payment service to integrate it with a database that is already up and running with a stack.

### 7.4.5  *The Payment service layer*

The Payment service depends on the database layer because it stores payment information for specific orders. To run the Payment service, we will need a Docker image built during the test container startup process, but we don't have a Dockerfile yet. In a Dockerfile, we express which parent Docker image will be used, and, in our case, we have two parent images: one for compilation and one for runtime. This type of build is called a *multistage build*, which we will cover in detail in chapter 8. For now, it is enough to know we use a Golang base image to build the payment project and a scratch image and payment executable to run the application.

You can navigate the payment folder and create a Dockerfile with the following content:

```
FROM golang:1.18 AS builder       ◁—— The builder name is alias.
WORKDIR /usr/src/app       ◁—┐
COPY . .                      └— Changes the working directory
RUN CGO_ENABLED=0 GOOS=linux go build -a -installsuffix cgo -o payment
➠ ./cmd/main.go       ◁—┐
                         └— Builds the binary executable

FROM scratch                                    ┌— Copies the binary from
COPY --from=builder /usr/src/app/payment ./payment   ◁—┤ the builder stage
CMD ["./payment"]       ◁—┐
                          └— The payment executable is an entry point.
```

Copies the source code of the payment

We also need some configurations in the environment variables: application port, database URL, and so forth. You can append the following service definition for the Payment service to the docker-compose.yml file as follows:

```
version: "3.9"
services:
  mysql:
    ...
  payment:              ┌— Depends on running
    depends_on:    ◁—┘ the mysql service
      mysql:
        condition: service_healthy       ┌— Dockerfile location
    build: ../../payment/    ◁—————┘ for the payment
    environment:
      APPLICATION_PORT: 8081
      ENV: "development"
      DATA_SOURCE_URL: "root:s3cr3t@tcp(mysql:3306)/
➠ payments?charset=utf8mb4&parseTime=True&loc=Local"
```

**Required configurations**

We can now continue with the Order service.

### 7.4.6 *The Order service layer*

The Order service definition is almost the same as the Payment service, except it has an additional configuration in the environment: a port exposed for our test suite to access. The only difference between the payment and order Dockerfile is the binary executable name:

```
FROM golang:1.18 AS builder
WORKDIR /usr/src/app
COPY . .
RUN CGO_ENABLED=0 GOOS=linux go build -a -installsuffix cgo -o order
➠ ./cmd/main.go

FROM scratch
COPY --from=builder /usr/src/app/order ./order
CMD ["./order"]
```

From the order folder, add this content to the Dockerfile. The service definition of the Order service is as follows:

```
version: "3.9"
services:
  mysql:
    ...
  payment:
    ...
  order:
    depends_on:
      mysql:
        condition: service_healthy
    build: ../../order/
    ports:
        "8080:8080"          ◁──┐ The test suite will
                                 │ use this port.
    environment:
      APPLICATION_PORT: 8080
      ENV: "development"
      DATA_SOURCE_URL: "root:s3cr3t@tcp(mysql:3306)/
        ➥ orders?charset=utf8mb4&parseTime=True&loc=Local"
      PAYMENT_SERVICE_URL: "localhost:8081"
```

**User payment gRPC connection** — points to `PAYMENT_SERVICE_URL: "localhost:8081"`

**The test suite will use this port.** — points to `"8080:8080"`

Now that we added the Order service definition, we can see how to use the docker-compose.yml file within our test suite.

### 7.4.7   *Running tests against the stack*

We will use the same test suite strategy here that we did with integration tests, and the application stack will be provisioned in the SetupSuite section. Here, we will have Docker Compose a reference (testcontainers.LocalDockerCompose), which will be available to the suite via the test suite struct (CreateOrderTestSuite). We will have only one test to test order creation flow during which we will create an order gRPC client to call Create and Get endpoints. Once we finish the test, the application stack will be destroyed in the TearDownSuite section. We can start by creating a file with the name create_order_e2e_test.go under the e2e folder and add the following struct:

```
type CreateOrderTestSuite struct {
    suite.Suite
    compose *testcontainers.LocalDockerCompose
}
```

**Suite dependency to use via the receiver function** — points to `suite.Suite`

**Docker Compose reference** — points to `compose *testcontainers.LocalDockerCompose`

In the SetupSuite section, we will use the e2e/resources/docker-compose.yml file we prepared previously for the Docker Compose up operation through test containers, as follows:

```
func (c *CreateOrderTestSuite) SetupSuite() {
    composeFilePaths := []string{"resources/docker-compose.yml"}
    identifier := strings.ToLower(uuid.New().String())

    compose := testcontainers.NewLocalDockerCompose(composeFilePaths,
      ➥ identifier)
    c.compose = compose
    execError := compose.
```

**docker-compose.yml we just prepared** — points to `composeFilePaths := []string{"resources/docker-compose.yml"}`

**Sets shared Docker compose reference** — points to `c.compose = compose`

**Randomized docker-compose file name** — points to `identifier`

```
        WithCommand([]string{"up", "-d"}).
        Invoke()          ◄─────┐ Equals docker-compose up -d
    err := execError.Error
    if err != nil {
        log.Fatalf("Could not run compose stack: %v", err)
    }
}
```

docker-compose up operation, which causes application stack creation, will be executed first. Our stack is ready and will create a gRPC connection to the Order service, which lives in the Docker container. We will do two things here:

- Verify there is no error after order creation.
- Get order details and verify fields with the ones we provided during the order creation.

Add the following test after the SetupSuite section:

```
func (c *CreateOrderTestSuite) Test_Should_Create_Order() {
    var opts []grpc.DialOption                              localhost:8080
    opts = append(opts,                                     goes to the
     grpc.WithTransportCredentials(insecure.NewCredentials()))  Order service
    conn, err := grpc.Dial("localhost:8080", opts...)  ◄─── in the stack.
    if err != nil {
        log.Fatalf("Failed to connect order service. Err: %v", err)
    }

    defer conn.Close()
                                              ┌─ Initializes Order
    orderClient := order.NewOrderClient(conn)  ◄─┘ gRPC client
    createOrderResponse, errCreate :=
  ➡  orderClient.Create(context.Background(), &order.CreateOrderRequest{
        UserId: 23,
        OrderItems: []*order.OrderItem{
            {
                ProductCode: "CAM123",
                Quantity:    3,
                UnitPrice:   1.23,
            },
        },
    }))
    c.Nil(errCreate)     ◄───── Verifies there is no error

    getOrderResponse, errGet := orderClient.Get(context.Background(),
  ➡  &order.GetOrderRequest{OrderId: createOrderResponse.OrderId})
    c.Nil(errGet)
    c.Equal(int64(23), getOrderResponse.UserId)
    orderItem := getOrderResponse.OrderItems[0]
    c.Equal(float32(1.23), orderItem.UnitPrice)
    c.Equal(int32(3), orderItem.Quantity)
    c.Equal("CAM123", orderItem.ProductCode)
}
```

Example order request annotation points to `})` line.

After success or failure, we need to shut the application stack down so as not to consume extra resources. We can do that in the `TearDownSuite` phase by using the Docker Compose reference and invoking the following shutdown operation:

```go
func (c *CreateOrderTestSuite) TearDownSuite() {
    execError := c.compose.
        WithCommand([]string{"down"}).
        Invoke()                        ◁────── Equals Docker Compose down
    err := execError.Error
    if err != nil {
        log.Fatalf("Could not shutdown compose stack: %v", err)
    }
}
```

As a final step, we can add a runner section to run the entire test:

```go
func TestCreateOrderTestSuite(t *testing.T) {
    suite.Run(t, new(CreateOrderTestSuite))
}
```

Our end-to-end test is almost ready; we just need to add the Order service client as a dependency to the e2e project via the following command:

```
go get github.com/huseyinbabal/microservices-proto/golang/order
```

Now you can use `NewOrderClient` and other order-related resources for your test. After all, you should have a folder structure, as shown in figure 7.7.

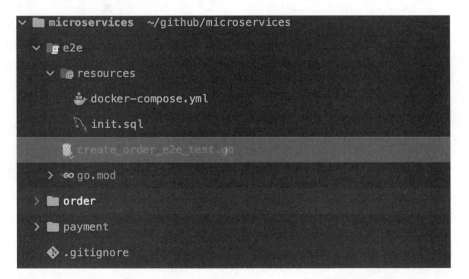

**Figure 7.7   End-to-end module structure**

You can now navigate to the e2e folder and execute the following test command to see how it works:

```
go test -run "^TestCreateOrderTestSuite$"
```

Notice we provide a regex to test the run command and start executing from `TestCreateOrderTestSuite`, the test suite runner.

To wrap up the end-to-end test, we simply run our application stack and run our tests against it, thanks to Testcontainers providing a good abstraction for Docker Compose that lets us run our stack via service definitions. This kind of test may take longer because it provisions a real system to verify features. Now that we have seen all the major test strategies for microservice architecture, let's look at how we can measure the coverage of our tests for the entire application.

## 7.5 Test coverage

The test coverage operation's primary motivation is to understand the missing test cases for production code. Code coverage is a strategy to detect how much of the application's entire codebase is covered by tests. Golang has very good built-in features for testing, and coverage can be automatically handled during test execution with the `-cover` parameter:

```
go test -cover ./…
```

Once you execute this command, you can see the coverage information for each package among test execution status:

```
ok
➥ github.com/huseyinbabal/microservices/order/internal/application/core/a
➥ pi       0.274s  coverage: 93.3% of statements
```

At the end of the line, you can see the coverage information of that package, which mostly describes your confidence level in the codebase (more coverage means you know your codebase better), and you can refactor your codebase with fewer problems. It is simple to see the coverage information for your tests, but let's look at how we can see the distribution of this coverage under a package.

### 7.5.1 Coverage information

With the `-cover` parameter, you can see the percentage of each package in the output. Completing the following steps shows a detailed report to drill down files, functions, and so on:

1  Redirect the coverage output to a file.
2  Use a built-in coverage tool to convert it to an HTML file.

You can use the following command to redirect detailed coverage information to a file:

```
go test -coverprofile=coverage.out
```

This will save coverage information into the coverage.out file, and then we are ready to pass this file to the following command to generate an HTML report.

```
go tool cover -html=coverage.out
```

`coverage.out` is provided via the `-html` option, which should generate an HTML report. In a modern automated environment, we are not interested in coverage reports in HTML format, but the coverage.out file can be passed to modern tools in our CI pipeline to maintain code quality for our repository. Now let's look at a brief introduction for using tests and coverages in a CI flow in our environment.

### 7.5.2    *Testing in a CI pipeline*

Continuous integration (CI) is a special automation that aims to integrate code changes. Those code changes can trigger testing and artifact generation, such as a Docker image or JAR file, to verify changes or build an artifact after changes are already approved. As a more concrete example, if you create a pull request (PR) in GitHub, CI can trigger a set of actions to calculate coverage and do some static code analysis to verify the code changes for maintaining quality. Once you merge this PR into the main branch, the CI can trigger a Docker image build operation with a special tag to use in application deployment. You can also configure rules, such as if the coverage is dropped under a certain threshold, the the PR check should fail. This will force the maintainer to revisit changes and add more tests to increase coverage. The more coverage you have, the more confidence you have during any change in the codebase. Figure 7.8 shows an overview of PR flow.

CI is powerful in maintaining code quality and reducing distraction while developing software. You can focus more on business logic development while CI handles checks and artifact generation for you.

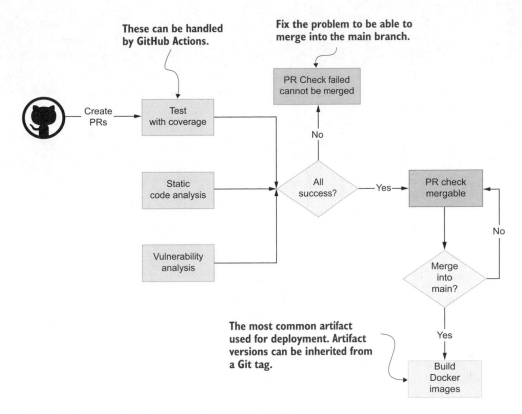

**Figure 7.8   PR flow with checks and artifact generation**

## Summary

- Testing is important to save time and money, and to maintain code quality, which results in almost bug-free applications in production.
- Unit testing is not designed for verifying the functions in a file; it is mostly helpful when you want to test scenarios in a file. A function can have one or more scenarios based on the conditional statements inside it. A SUT gives the exact place in the code base you are running your test against.
- We can use integration tests to test two modules to verify they are well integrated. The most popular example is testing a data layer with a real database. Test containers are beneficial here.
- Suites work well for defining requirements before tests and destroying required components after tests. Setup and TearDown are very powerful in integration tests because we create the DB adaptor before the test and destroy it once we finish.
- End-to-end tests can contain all the available services in your environment because you test a flow from beginning to end.

- The test pyramid is used to explain the distribution of test percentages for each test type. Unit testing has a bigger percentage of the pyramid since it is preferred, mostly to get faster feedback and reduce the cost of the testing infrastructure.
- Test outputs and test coverage can be used in the CI pipeline to verify PRs.

# Deployment 8

## This chapter covers

- Building Docker images for gRPC services
- Understanding the components of Kubernetes
- Maintaining certificates in Kubernetes to enable TLS communication between end user and services
- The motivation behind deployment strategies

Microservices architecture is built on top of a distributed system in which you can see many services, standalone CronJobs, third-party dependencies, and so on. Since there are many challenges in such an environment, it is important to build cloud-native applications. Container technologies like Docker help generate cloud-native artifacts from those application source codes. In the same way, Kubernetes, an open source container orchestration platform, helps deploy artifacts in an environment in which most of the cloud components, such as a load balancer, disk, and networking, are abstracted. In this chapter, we will learn how to build artifacts within the CI (continuous integration) pipeline and deploy gRPC microservices to Kubernetes in the CD (continuous deployment) pipeline.

> **About code examples in this chapter**
>
> In chapter 4, we started coding our services, and in the code in this chapter is based on what we implemented in chapters 4 and 5. The examples in this chapter are complete, and you can build Docker images and deploy any of them to Kubernetes. We will continue to extend it to see how CD works.

## 8.1    *Docker*

Docker is a platform that helps you to build and package your application and its dependencies, as well as deploy it seamlessly. (See this book to learn more: https://www.manning.com/books/docker-in-action-second-edition.) Here, I will skip the basics and provide practical information. Building a Docker image for a Go application is easy since we simply add a Go binary executable into the Docker image, and it already has all the dependencies we need inside it. This executable will be the container's entry point, a runnable instance of the Docker image, so that it will launch our application whenever you run a container. To better understand this process, let's look at how we can build a Docker image for our microservices.

### 8.1.1    *Building images*

Building a Docker image has two steps:

1. Prepare a Dockerfile.
2. Execute `docker build -t <image_name>`.

In the Dockerfile, a line should start with the FROM keyword to state our application's parent image. In Go, there are different dependencies for compile time and runtime. For example, we need to be able to run `go build …` to generate a Go binary executable, but once we build it, we no longer need the Go distribution in the container runtime. We can provide a generated Go executable binary as an entry point to the Docker container. Separating compile time and runtime dependencies in Docker images is the process of creating *multistage builds* in Docker (see https://docs.docker.com/develop/develop-images/multistage-build/). In the example that follows, a Golang Docker image will be the parent image that executes the `go build` command, and we will pass a generated artifact to the next stage, which uses a scratch Docker image as the parent. The scratch image is a special one that you cannot pull or run as a standalone container but that you can use as a parent and provide an executable as an entry point:

```
FROM golang:1.18 AS builder        ⊲──┐  Uses the Golang Docker
WORKDIR /usr/src/app                  │  image as parent
COPY . .                  ⊲──────  Copies Go source code to the Docker image
RUN CGO_ENABLED=0 GOOS=linux go build -a -installsuffix cgo -o order
 ➥ ./cmd/main.go   ⊲───┐
                        │  Builds a go binary executable       Copies a generated artifact from
FROM scratch                                                   the first stage to second one
COPY --from=builder /usr/src/app/order ./order   ⊲───────┘
CMD ["./order"]                     ⊲──────  Orders a gRPC server as an entry point
```

Now you can create a Dockerfile under the Order service in the microservices project (`order/Dockerfile`) and add this content. We will soon use this to prepare our Docker image. Notice that you can create one more Dockerfile for the Payment service. Just replace the order with a payment, then put that in the payment/Dockerfile file (figure 8.1).

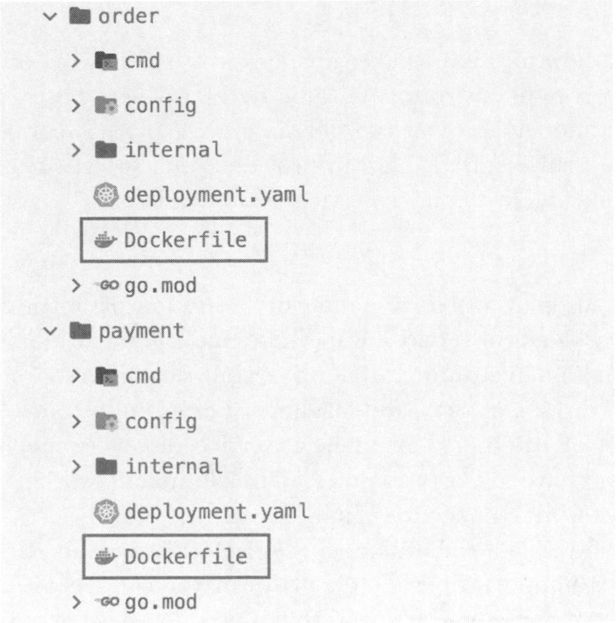

```
∨ 📁 order
   > 📁 cmd
   > 📁 config
   > 📁 internal
      ⚙ deployment.yaml
      🐳 Dockerfile
   > 🐹 go.mod
∨ 📁 payment
   > 📁 cmd
   > 📁 config
   > 📁 internal
      ⚙ deployment.yaml
      🐳 Dockerfile
   > 🐹 go.mod
```

**Figure 8.1   Dockerfile in each service folder**

Since we have a Dockerfile for each service, we are ready to build Docker images as follows:

```
docker build -t order .
```

If you execute this command while you are in the order folder, the current folder will be in Docker context (since that is the location of the Dockerfile) and a local Docker image will be built for you, but it should be published to a remote registry, a storage system in which you can store your Docker images so that Kubernetes can pull them. The most popular Docker registries for production environments follow but in this chapter, we will not use registries; we will copy them to Kubernetes cluster nodes to have faster development feedback:

- https://hub.docker.com/
- https://quay.io/
- https://cloud.google.com/container-registry
- https://aws.amazon.com/ecr/

You can also install the on-premises version of Docker registries in your network for better performance during pull and push operations. If you are using Docker Hub as your Docker image registry, you can use the following command to push your images after you tag them:

```
docker tag order huseyinbabal/order:1.0.0
docker push huseyinbabal/order:1.0.0
```

Now that we understand how to build Docker images for our Go microservices let's get familiar with our deployment environment, Kubernetes. Docker registry providers require a valid authentication token you can get via a `docker login` command. Of course, in the Kubernetes environment, we can provide a pull secret since running the Docker command while deploying microservices is not feasible.

## 8.2   Kubernetes

Kubernetes (i.e., k8s) is an open source container orchestration platform that helps manage containerized workloads or services. Kubernetes has a good abstraction layer, a virtualized logical operating environment that utilizes physical hardware infrastructure components such as disks, networks, and machines. For example, once Kubernetes is deployed on a set of machines, an internal service discovery mechanism is provided so that you don't have to worry about IP addresses in a networking context. Microservices can interact with their service names.

Now that we understand what a Kubernetes cluster is, let's look at its core components. Since Kubernetes is a popular open source platform, you can see it in almost all cloud providers; you can go to their consoles and spin it up with one click. In the same way, you can include Kubernetes cluster installation in your infrastructure as a code pipeline to provision clusters with Terraform or other cloud provider–specific SDKs such as `eksctl` (http://mng.bz/Gye8). In the cloud environment, you can use AKS, Azure-managed Kubernetes; EKS, AWS-managed Kubernetes; or GKE, Google Cloud–managed Kubernetes. If your services are on bare metal servers, Kubespray is also an option (https://github.com/kubernetes-sigs/kubespray).

### 8.2.1   Kubernetes architecture

A Kubernetes cluster is a distributed system made from a machine set that contains primarily containerized workloads. Those nodes are divided into control plane nodes and worker nodes. The *control plane* is the brain of the Kubernetes cluster, and it has mission-critical components to manage resources in the Kubernetes environment. Those resources are specific to Kubernetes, but they manage a containerized application under the hood. *Worker nodes* contain system components like `kubelet` and workloads like pods, the minimum deployable unit in Kubernetes (see figure 8.2).

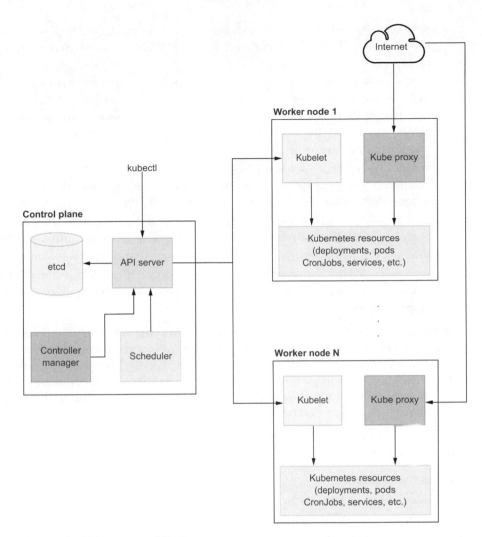

**Figure 8.2 Kubernetes architecture**

Let's look at a simple explanation of each component:

- Kubectl—This is the command-line application for Kubernetes, that allows you to manage your resources and Kubernetes cluster nodes. Its primary responsibility is providing a simple interface to the end user while interacting with the API server in the control plane.
- *API server*—This is the Kubernetes cluster API endpoint that provides unified access to end users for Kubernetes management. You can manage your Kubernetes resources or maintain Kubernetes nodes through this component with the help of kubectl.

- *Scheduler*—Whenever you try to deploy a pod (the minimum deployable unit in Kubernetes), it will be scheduled to an available node based on resource requirements.
- *Controller manager*—This component manages the controller processes available in Kubernetes, such as `ReplicationController`. Whenever there is a change for a resource definition, `ReplicationController` detects it and applies it to a specific resource to create the desired state. This can be a replica count change, Docker image change, and so on.
- `etcd`—This is used to store resource states in the Kubernetes environment. Whenever you create a pod, the metadata is stored in `etcd` first, and then the scheduler handles the remaining part to schedule it to the available node.
- `kubelet`—This worker node component is in contact with the API server, and its primary responsibility is to track the state of pod specification. It continuously checks the pod, ensures underlying containers are healthy, and reports to control plane.
- `kube-proxy`—This component exposes services to the outside once they are needed, allowing each service to communicate through a special internal discovery system.

NOTE  You will see many examples related to Kubernetes resource operations for deploying microservices. You can try all of them locally using `Minikube`, a local Kubernetes cluster that helps you learn and try out Kubernetes (https:// minikube.sigs.k8s.io/docs/start/). You can also use `kubectl`, a command-line tool that allows you to run commands against a Kubernetes cluster (https:// kubernetes.io/docs/tasks/tools/#kubectl).

Now that we understand the components of a Kubernetes cluster, let's look at what kind of resources are available and how they work.

### 8.2.2  Kubernetes resources

You can't deploy containers to the Kubernetes cluster directly because there is an abstraction on top—a *pod*, a minimum deployable unit that helps you define the containerized application and its environmental configurations and claim disks, once they are needed. We talk about specifications like pod specification: YAML definitions that contain information about cloud-native applications. It has three mandatory fields: `apiVersion`, `kind`, and `spec`. `apiVersion` maintains versioning inside the API server. `kind` is for defining the resource type, such as `Pod`, `Deployment`, `Cronjob`, `Service`, etc. `spec` is the most important specification because it contains the metadata of the application you want to run on the Kubernetes environment. In this section, you can define the characteristics of a workload as follows:

- You can specify the Docker image with its version.
- You can either statically pass environment variables with their values or pass them from a Kubernetes `Secret` or `ConfigMap`. `Secret`s store confidential values in `base64` encoded format, and `ConfigMap` maintains configurations in a key-value format.

- You can define how much memory or CPU reservation you need for your application.
- You can specify what the behavior should do when the application crashes.

Let's look at real-life microservices examples by diving deep into widely used Kubernetes resources we can use during application deployment.

### 8.2.3   *Eagle view of microservices deployment*

Assume that we already have a Docker image for each microservice that we can run as a container by providing the minimum required configurations. If we use only Docker in our machine, we would run that service as follows:

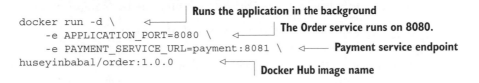

```
docker run -d \                    Runs the application in the background
    -e APPLICATION_PORT=8080 \     The Order service runs on 8080.
    -e PAYMENT_SERVICE_URL=payment:8081 \   Payment service endpoint
huseyinbabal/order:1.0.0           Docker Hub image name
```

In Kubernetes, instead of directly running a containerized application, we deploy a pod that encapsulates the container runtime. This might seem like an unnecessary encapsulation, but maybe you already know Kubernetes used the Docker engine as the default container runtime for a while, then removed it with the release of Kubernetes 1.24. If Kubernetes had a direct dependency on the Docker engine, it would be hard to migrate our Kubernetes workload if we wanted to upgrade to Kubernetes 1.24 from earlier releases. However, as you can see in figure 8.3, there are pods for the actual application workloads Kubernetes handles.

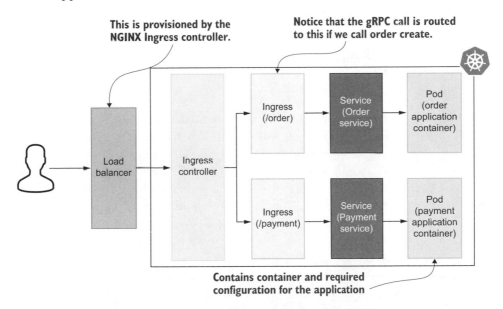

**Figure 8.3   High-level overview of Order and Payment service deployments**

By default, pods are closed boxes; if you want to expose them to the public internet, use `Services`, which help expose pods as an endpoint inside Kubernetes. If you access that endpoint with a particular path, you can use Ingress to define the path and mapped service to route traffic. Finally, suppose you want to make those paths available outside with automation. In that case, the Ingress controller creates a load balancer and points it to an `nginx` instance that contains all the pod Ingress configurations. Now that we understand the practical details behind Kubernetes resources, let's dive deep into each one and examine them with real-life examples.

### 8.2.4   *Pod*

In this section, we will write down our requirements to get the Order service up and running, then try to create pod specification by referring to its requirements:

- Docker image to be used as an entry point within a pod
- Application port value as an environment variable
- Payment service URL as an environment variable

```
apiVersion: v1
kind: Pod
metadata:
  name: order
spec:
  containers:
  - name: order
    image: huseyinbabal/order:1.0.0
    env:
      - name: APPLICATION_PORT
        value: "8080"
      - name: "PAYMENT_SERVICE_URL"
           value: "payment:8081"
```

If we save this as `order.yaml` and execute

```
kubectl apply -f order.yaml
```

`kubectl` will generate a payload using this YAML content and push it to the Kubernetes API server. The API server will save this metadata into a state store, `etcd` in our case; then it will be scheduled by the `kube-scheduler` onto an available node. After the `kube-scheduler` assigns this pod to a specific node, `kubelet` will pull the Docker image specified in the image filed and run the container with environment variables provided under the `env` section. We will use other Kubernetes resources, such as deployment and `Service`, but in general, the resource scheduling flow described is the same (see figure 8.4).

Figure 8.4 is a typical pod deployment flow with just one instance of a service. However, we may need more than one instance in real life for availability. Let's look at what kind of Kubernetes resources we can use for multiple instances of the same pod template.

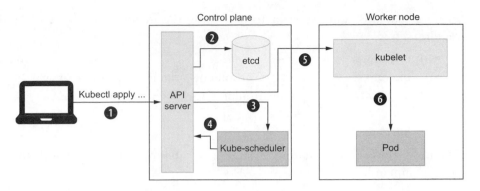

**Figure 8.4** `kubectl apply` **flow**

### 8.2.5 *Deployment*

A Kubernetes resource that ensures the specified number of Pod replicas are available at any time is called `ReplicaSet` (https://kubernetes.io/docs/concepts/workloads/controllers/replicaset/). For example, you can have three instances of the Order service, two instances of the Payment service, and one instance of the Shipping service based on your requirements. Even though you can use `ReplicaSet` to directly manage the instances of a given pod, it is suggested that you also use Deployment to cover other requirements such as updating a policy. For example, suppose you want to use `ReplicaSet` to deploy Order service `v1.0.0` and upgrade it to `v1.0.1`. In that case, you must create a new `ReplicaSet` with Order service `v1.0.1` and a downscale `ReplicaSet` with version `v1.0.0`. If you use deployment to manage your actual pods, you don't need to maintain `ReplicaSets`; you just need to update the image version, and deployment will handle the remainder for you. If you create a deployment with name `order-service`, deployment will create `Replicaset order-service-<replicaset-suffix>` and `ReplicaSet` will create `order-service-<replicaset-suffix>-<pod-suffix>` (see figure 8.5).

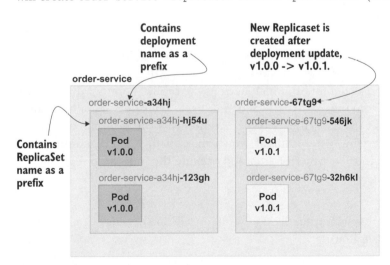

**Figure 8.5
Deployment,
ReplicaSet, and
pod relationship**

Assume that this time we want to deploy the Payment service with the following requirements:

- It contains a `v1.0.2` image.
- It has an `APPLICATION_PORT` environment variable with a value of `8081`.
- It has a `DATA_SOURCE_URL` environment variable with a value of `root:changeit@tcp (mysql:3306)/payments`.
- It has `two` replicas.

Then, we can use the following YAML file to submit to Kubernetes with the `kubectl apply` command:

```
apiVersion: apps/v1
kind: Deployment
metadata:
  name: payment      ◁——— Name of the deployment
  labels:
    app: payment     ◁——— Labels are good, especially for filtering.
spec:
  replicas: 2   ◁——— Two pod instances
  Selector:
    matchLabels:
      app: payment     ◁——— Applies to pods with those labels
  template:
    metadata:
      labels:
        app: payment     ◁——— Each pod instance will have these labels.
    spec:
      containers:
      - name: payment
        image: huseyinbabal/payment:v1.0.2
        env:
          - name: APPLICATION_PORT
            value: "8081"
          - name: DATA_SOURCE_URL
            value: "root:changeit@tcp(mysql:3306)/payments"
```

You can see the `labels` section in all kinds of Kubernetes resources, which are primarily used for grouping resources and to filter once that is needed. The `spec` section shows the `replicas` definition, which decides the replica count of pod instances, which are inherited from the template, as seen in the `template` field. Finally, in the inner `spec` section, you can see the actual pod specification that will be applied to all instances of the pod. To create a deployment, you can save this YAML content in a deployment.yaml file in the payment folder and execute the following:

```
kubectl apply -f deployment.yaml
```

You can verify this by getting the pod status and listing deployments, or get details of a specific pod, as follows:

```
kubectl get deployments
# or
kubectl get deployment payment -o yaml
```

We just created a deployment, and it also created the required `ReplicaSet` and pod. This pod contains the workload, the Payment service, in our case, but how can we access this service as an end user? Let's look at the possible ways to do this in Kubernetes.

### 8.2.6 *Service*

Once a pod is deployed on a worker node in Kubernetes, by default it cannot receive traffic from outside. To create outside exposure, you can use the `Service` resource, which acts like a gateway between the client and the actual pod in the Kubernetes environment. A client, which can be a public user, can also be inside Kubernetes. Both scenarios can be achieved with different Kubernetes `Service` types. For example, if you want to expose the Shipping service to Kubernetes internally, you can use the `ClusterIP` type of `Service`. If you expose it outside of Kubernetes, we have two options, `LoadBalancer` and `NodePort`. Let's look at examples to better understand the logic behind these types.

Once the `LoadBalancer` `Service` type is used, it provisions a load balancer based on cloud provider metadata. For example, if you create a `LoadBalancer` type `Service` in AWS, it can create an AWS load balancer. The Kubernetes cloud plugins handle this operation, and you don't need to deal with cloud provider internals because there is good abstraction in Kubernetes for this kind of operation. Once the `LoadBalancer` `Service` type is successfully created, you can use the newly created load balancer URL to access the pod behind that `Service`.

If we use the `NodePort` `Service` type, then the pod behind that `Service` will be available to the public through a specified port in the `Service` YAML definition. For this use case, you need to know the physical IP address of at least one of the worker nodes. Finally, you can access the pod by using its URL in the following format `<public_ip_of_worker_node>:<port_in_service_definition>`.

Assume we want to expose the Payment service we deployed in the previous section as a load balancer to the public user:

```
apiVersion: v1
kind: Service
metadata:
  name: payment
  labels:
    app: payment
spec:
  selector:
    app: payment          ◁─┐  Routes traffic to the pod with
  ports:                      the label "app: payment"
    - name: grpc   ◁──────  Named port
      port: 80   ◁───┐
                     │  Public port on the load balancer
```

```
        protocol: TCP        ◁──── Connection protocol
        targetPort: 8081     ◁──
┌─▷ type: LoadBalancer              Internal port of the Payment service
│
Creates a load balancer
```

Like other resources, `Service` has name and label fields for basic metadata. It also has a `spec` field for mapping a pod and `Service` using selectors. It also contains port information for routing traffic from a public user to a specific pod. You can also see a flow in which multiple `Services` route traffic to multiple pods using selectors (figure 8.6). Since we use the type `LoadBalancer` here, Kubernetes will create a load balancer in the cloud provider with its internal cloud plug-ins.

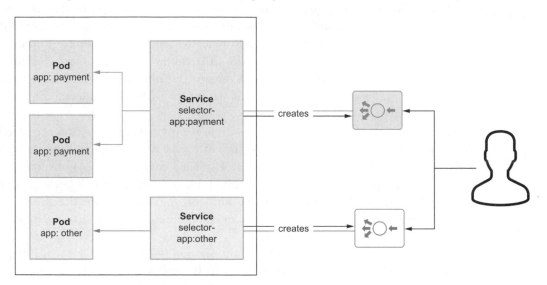

**Figure 8.6**  `Service` **type** `LoadBalancer`

The first load balancer is created by `Service` with the `app:payment` selector. That means the request to that load balancer will be routed to a pod with the label `app:payment`. In the same way, once a request is made to a second load balancer, it will be routed to a pod with the label `app:order` because a `Service` creates that load balancer with the selector `app:order`.

If we want to expose these two services to the public using `NodePort`, the following flow explains our use case: We simply bind a port in all worker nodes for a specific pod in this flow. It does not matter which worker node's IP address you use. If you use the `IP:port` pair, of which `IP` is one of the IP addresses of the worker nodes, the traffic will be routed to the correct pod, as shown in figure 8.7.

In `NodePort Service`, to access a specific service, refer to a port by visiting any worker node. As shown in figure 8.7, once a user requests the first worker node, the request is proxied to the second worker node since the pod behind the `Service` is

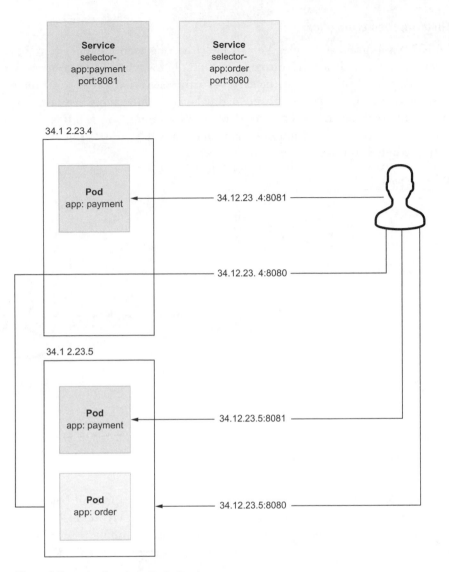

**Figure 8.7**  `Service` **type** `NodePort`

located in the second worker node. Notice that, with `NodePort` usage, you need to know the public IP addresses of the worker nodes if you are trying to access pods from outside of the Kubernetes network.

A specific pod can have outside exposure with `LoadBalancer` or `NodePort` service types. With `LoadBalancer`, a cloud load balancer is created, and with `NodePort`, a specified port is reserved for that service in worker nodes. Would it be valuable to create a `LoadBalancer` for each microservice to expose to the public? Let's answer this question by checking the internals of the Ingress controller.

### 8.2.7   *NGINX Ingress controller*

The NGINX Ingress controller helps you create one load balancer per Ingress controller and has a dedicated resource Ingress that helps traffic routing between the end user and a pod. If you create three `Services` with `LoadBalancer` type for three microservices, the controller will create three load balancers, one each. If you deploy the controller and create an Ingress resource for traffic routing, you will have just one load balancer instead of three. That one load balancer will be responsible for handling all the traffic between the end user and the pod.

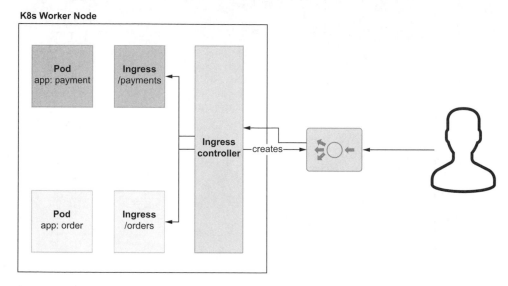

**Figure 8.8   NGINX Ingress controller**

NGINX Ingress plays key role in routing the traffic from the load balancer to actual pods. The logic behind this is very simple: whenever you create an Ingress resource, the Ingress controller detects this change and refreshes the nginx.conf file with new paths inside the controller. Let's look at the Ingress resource for the Order service:

```
apiVersion: networking.k8s.io/v1
kind: Ingress
metadata:
  annotations:
    kubernetes.io/ingress.class: nginx
    nginx.ingress.kubernetes.io/backend-protocol: GRPC    ⟵── States the gRPC backend
 ┌─▷ nginx.ingress.kubernetes.io/ssl-redirect: "true"
    cert-manager.io/cluster-issuer: selfsigned-issuer    ⟵── Certificate automation
  name: order
spec:
  rules:
    - http:
        paths:
```

**gRPC, by default works on HTTPS.**

```
        - path: /Order      ⟵——— Context path for the Order gRPC
          pathType: Prefix
          backend:
            service:
              name: order
              port:
                number: 8080
    tls:
      - hosts:
          - ingress.local   ⟵——— Authorized domain for TLS
```

The Ingress resource has name and label fields like other Kubernetes resources, and most of the configurations are done via the annotation section. This is followed by some rule patterns in which the `route` operation is applied to a specific path (e.g., backend protocol, certificate issuer, and SSL redirect).

To deploy the Ingress controller, you can use the helm package manager (https://helm.sh/) to deploy the `nginx-ingress` chart:

```
                                                       Adds the required
                                                       repository for the chart
helm repo add ingress-nginx https://kubernetes.github.io/ingress-nginx  ⟵———┐
helm repo  update #B
helm install nginx-ingress ingress-nginx/ingress-nginx   ⟵———┐
                                                       Installs resources
Updates the repository index                           via the chart
```

This will simply deploy an `nginx` instance inside a pod, creating a load balancer. Whenever you request this load balancer, it goes through the NGINX pod, which also contains `nginx.conf`. NGINX configurations are rerendered whenever there is a change for any Ingress resource.

In sum, we deployed a pod that contains the actual workload, in our case, any microservice. Then we learned how to manage replicas of that pod and automatically handle image updates. We used `Service` to expose the pod to the public using `Service` with the `LoadBalancer`, `NodePort`, and `ClusterIP` options. Finally, we tried to understand the benefits of using the NGINX Ingress controller, which provisions a load balancer and then uses Ingress resources to configure routing for public access. Now that we understand how the public traffic reaches the pod in the Kubernetes environment, let's look at how TLS certification automation is handled, as we also need it for Ingress resources.

## 8.3 Certificate management

We already addressed how TLS-enabled communication works for gRPC microservices and followed a step-by-step explanation of TLS certification generation for secure gRPC communication. In this section, we will automate this process via cert-manager (https://cert-manager.io/docs/), a tool that helps us obtain, renew, then use certificates in the Kubernetes environment. cert-manager provides custom CRDs (custom resource definitions), which are responsible for certificate-related resources and for integrating third parties to obtain certificates. Vault (https://www.vaultproject.io/)

and Let's Encrypt (https://letsencrypt.org/) are examples of cert-manager integrations, but we will use a self-signed certificate to explain concepts in the local Kubernetes cluster. Let's look at the custom resources cert-manager provides and apply the integration to see it in action for the Order service.

### 8.3.1   Installation

cert-manager contains custom resources for generating and injecting certificates to specific workloads. Installation will create custom resources in Kubernetes that we can use in our deployment pipeline. There are several options to install cert-manager: Helm, Operator, or `kubectl apply`. Let's use Helm:

```
helm repo add jetstack https://charts.jetstack.io     ◁──── Repo for cert-manager
helm repo update                              ◁──┐
helm install \                                   │ Updates the repository index
  cert-manager jetstack/cert-manager \
  --namespace cert-manager \
  --create-namespace \     ◁──── Creates a namespace if it does not exist
  --version v1.10.0 \
  --set installCRDs=true     ◁──── Installs all CRDs
```

You can verify and see all the available CRDs installed via cert-manager as follows:

```
kubectl get crds
```

As a result, you will see six CRDs: `CertificateRequests`, `Certificates`, `Challenges`, `ClusterIssuers`, `Issuers`, and `Orders`. We will focus on `ClusterIssuers`. Let's create a `ClusterIssuer` to handle the self-signed certification flow, which is very handy for local development.

### 8.3.2   ClusterIssuer

I find this resource name (`ClusterIssuer`) significant because when you want to use a certificate for TLS communication, you must "issue a certificate." `ClusterIssuer` does that for you cluster wide. You would use the following resource to create a self-signed certificate in a Kubernetes cluster:

```
apiVersion: cert-manager.io/v1
kind: ClusterIssuer
metadata:
  name: selfsigned-issuer
spec:
  selfSigned: {}
```

As always, save this content in cluster-issuer.yaml and use following to create this resource in Kubernetes cluster:

```
kubectl apply -f cluster-issuer.yaml
```

You can verify creation with this command:

```
kubectl get clusterissuers -o wide selfsigned-issuer
```

Now that we have a valid certificate in the Kubernetes cluster, let's use it in one of our Ingress resources.

### 8.3.3   Certificate usage in Ingress

The self-signed certificate we created is only authorized for local development and uses Ingress's `.local` domain name. Add the following record to /etc/hosts:

```
ingress.local 127.0.0.1
```

We use `127.0.0.1` here since, at the end of this section, we will make our first microservices request via a tunnel provided by the `minikube tunnel` command. Notice that we already visited the Ingress configuration for the Order service in in section 8.2.7; now we will extend it to configure TLS communication:

```
apiVersion: networking.k8s.io/v1
kind: Ingress
metadata:
  annotations:
    kubernetes.io/ingress.class: nginx
    nginx.ingress.kubernetes.io/backend-protocol: GRPC
    nginx.ingress.kubernetes.io/ssl-redirect: "true"
    cert-manager.io/cluster-issuer: selfsigned-issuer   ⟵──┘ Configures a certificate
  name: order                                                 for this Ingress
spec:
  rules:
    - http:
        paths:
          - path: /Order
            pathType: Prefix
            backend:
              service:
                name: order
                port:
                  number: 8080
  tls:
    - hosts:                          │ TLS configuration is
        - ingress.local   ⟵──────────┘ authorized for this domain.
```

As you can see, certificate configuration is handled by annotations, a widely used technique to extend resources' capabilities. Now we have certificates in place, they are issued, and Ingress is configured to work with them. Notice that the certificates are not by default available to any client. Let's look at how to handle certificate management on the client side to create a secure connection between the gRPC client and the gRPC server.

### 8.3.4    *Certificates on the client side*

minikube has an available command, `minikube tunnel`, that creates a proxy through 127.0.0.1 so that whenever you request 127.0.0.1, that request will be proxied to the Ingress controller inside minikube. Let's create a tunnel:

```
minikube tunnel
```

Open your browser and request https://ingress.local to see if you will get a certificate issued. You can simply click the padlock/info icon in the browser next to the insecure message and download the certificate. If you double-click on that certificate, it will prompt you to install the certificate into your key chain. Refer to http://mng.bz/zXZg for detailed steps on how to collect the certificate from the browser.

You should see a secure connection after installing the certificate. We are requesting a browser, but this is not a gRPC communication. To make a gRPC call, we can still use `grpcurl` and provide the .proto files to understand what kind of methods are available to `grpcurl` for the requested service:

```
grpcurl -import-path /path/to/order -proto order.proto ingress.local:443
➥ Order.Create
```

In previous chapters, we handled those .proto files; locate them on your computer and pass the folder's full path to the `grpcurl` command with the parameter `-import-path` and `-proto` file. Now `grpcurl` knows the methods to construct correct request metadata for the gRPC call. Notice that we don't need .proto files for the programmatic approach. For example, if you want to call the Order service via a Go client, adding .proto files as a dependency and using client functions to call specific services is enough.

We started with creating a pod and exposing it to the public via the `Service` resource. Using the `LoadBalancer Service` type seemed straightforward, but it may not be efficient for microservices because we end up with lots of load balancers, which is not cost-effective. Then we used the Ingress controller to handle routing with Ingress resources, and the controller became our single-entry point as a load balancer. Finally, we managed our certificates with a cert manager, as gRPC only works with HTTPS over HTTP/2. Now that we understand how to complete a simple deployment into a Kubernetes cluster, let's look at advanced deployment strategies we can use in microservices deployments.

## 8.4    *Deployment strategies*

Deploying to Kubernetes is not a one-time operation; it is an operation that is integrated into a CD pipeline that updates the container image artifact once we want to make changes in the actual workload. This is mostly done by updating the image version, but it can also be done by updating environment variables of pod containers or by changing replicas of a deployment. You will hear about `RollingUpdate`, `Blue-Green`, or `Canary` deployment while searching the internals of Kubernetes deployment. Let's look at each of these deployment strategies with real-life examples.

### 8.4.1 *RollingUpdate*

RollingUpdate is a deployment strategy in which a new ReplicaSet is created for the new version, and the old ReplicaSet is gradually removed until the new one has the correct number of replicas. This is the default behavior of a deployment in Kubernetes (http://mng.bz/0KQW). Assume that we have huseyinbabal/order:1.0.0 in our deployment, and you want to deploy a new version of 1.1.0. You can trigger a rolling update with the following command:

```
kubectl set image deployment/order order=order:1.1.0
```

Here, we simply update the deployment and change the order container to use a new image (figure 8.9).

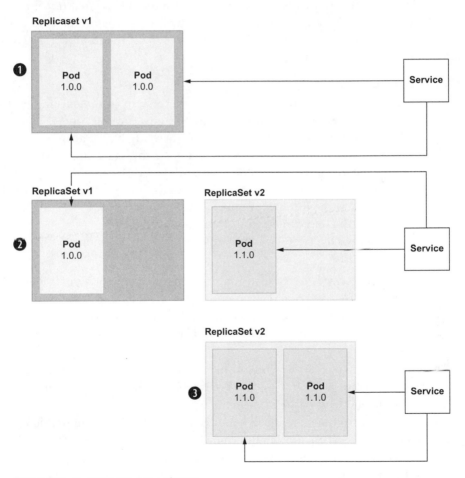

**Figure 8.9** RollingUpdate **phases**

As you can see in figure 8.9, `RollingUpdate` is completed in three steps:

1.  Service proxies traffic to two pod instances under `ReplicaSet` v1.
2.  Once the image is updated for deployment, it creates `Replicaset` v2 and assigns a new pod to this `ReplicaSet`.
3.  Meanwhile, one pod is removed from `ReplicaSet` v1 because having two replicas works for us. `Service` proxies traffic to the pod in `ReplicaSet` v1 and `ReplicaSet` v2.
4.  `ReplicaSet` v2 has two available pods, and all the pods under `ReplicaSet` v1 are removed. Finally, `Service` proxies all the traffics to the pods under `ReplicaSet` v2, which contains a new Docker image version.

It does not take much time to complete a `RollingUpdate`, and in this interval, v1 pod and v2 pod may be available at the same time. Here, you can clearly see that it is crucial to develop a system that is always backward compatible so that once we roll back our deployment to v1, the system should continue to work without any data inconsistency or downtime. Now that we understand `RollingUpdate`, let's look at the next strategy: `Blue-Green` deployment.

### 8.4.2  *Blue-Green Deployment*

In this type of deployment strategy, there are two versions of the existing system, and whenever a deployment occurs on one of the systems, the old one becomes deprecated by routing traffic to the new system. We currently have Payment Service v1 in production and plan to deploy v2 soon. However, this time it will not be like an almost-instant update like in `RollingUpdate`; v2 will be prepared in advance, and traffic will be switched to v2 after everything is taken care of. In this case, we start with `Green` (v1), and when v2 is deployed it is `Blue` at the beginning, but after a while will be `Green`. You can see the deployment transitions in figure 8.10.

Figure 8.10 shows the overall picture of blue-green deployment, but what happens under the hood is this:

- Remember, once we create an Ingress controller, it provisions a load balancer, and we add Ingress resources behind this controller using the Ingress name.
- For the blue environment, an additional Ingress controller can be deployed, and Ingress v2 can be involved behind the load balancer created by the new Ingress controller.
- The current state is our domain has a record pointing to the initial load balancer (green), and once we feel confident, we simply update the record value as the second load balancer.
- Once we introduce a new version, it is deployed behind the first load balancer and becomes green after an internal check.
- Most of the time, blue environments are accessible from the internal network so that they can be tested by internal employees or a particular group of testers.

    This deployment strategy is smoother since we simply change the load balancer switch. However, since we duplicate the existing system entirely as v2, it will introduce an additional cost.

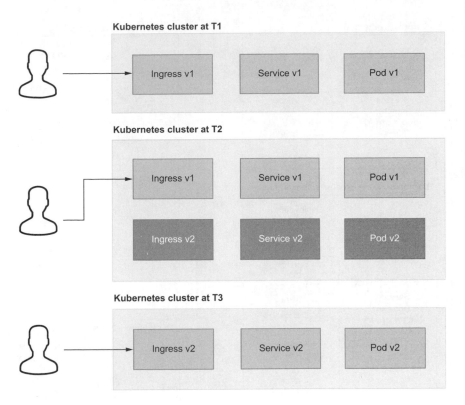

**Figure 8.10   Blue-green deployment**

Now that we understand Blue-Green deployment, let's look at canary deployment.

### 8.4.3   *Canary deployment*

Remember that a Service resource is designed to expose a pod as an endpoint internally or publicly to users. The Service–pod relationship is handled by selectors in the Service resource so that Service uses a selector field to find available pods filtered by the logic inside the selector. In canary deployment, there is always one service, but this time an additional deployment is created with new data (e.g., a new Docker image) but with the same selector. Then, requests are distributed between v1 and v2 pods. In canary deployment, this percentage is gradually changed until all the replicas become available in the new deployment and the old one is downscaled to zero (figure 8.11).

In figure 8.11, you can see the transitions for canary deployment, which are simply a summary of gradually increasing the possibility of seeing the newly deployed feature while deprecating the old deployment. We need a second deployment here with the same selector so that once the request reaches the load balancer, it will be routed to a pod by selectors. Canary deployment is widely used, especially for collecting feedback from end users by enabling an experimental feature to a subset of customers instead of overwriting the current production.

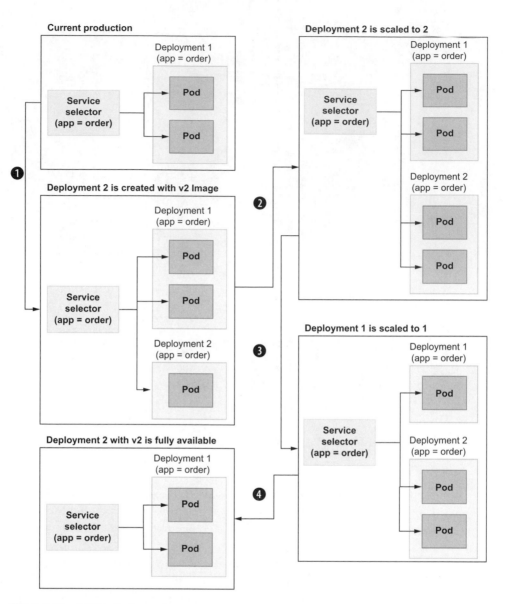

**Figure 8.11   Canary deployment**

### 8.4.4   *Final thoughts on deployment*

To better understand deployments, we used a traditional approach to deploy a work-load to the Kubernetes environment by kubectl. However, multiple options exist to automate this process within the GitOps context. ArgoCD (https://argo-cd.readthedocs .io/en/stable/) and FluxCD (https://fluxcd.io/) are famous examples of GitOps nota-tion; you can connect them to the repository, and whenever you push a change to this repository, they handle deployments for you.

We saw how to use cert-manager for local development to set up a proper self-signed certificate generation and inject it to enable TLS for Ingress resources. cert-manager is so powerful you can integrate it with well-known certificate managers, such as Let's Encrypt and Vault. You can even integrate cert-manager with Cloudflare so that TLS will be handled on Cloudflare, and necessary configurations will be applied to it. These kinds of seamless integrations are important for implementing business logic and not disturbing manual infrastructure operations.

If you want to inject confidential data into workloads like pods, you can use Kubernetes secrets. You can even use `ExternalSecrets` (https://external-secrets.io/v0.7.0/) to maintain your secrets in a third-party tool.

## Summary

- Building a cloud-native application is important for productivity, as this helps you ship products within containerized applications.
- Kubernetes has good abstraction on top of cloud technologies in which you manage components through resource declaration. Kubernetes will take care of container orchestration and create necessary components in the cloud.
- Deployment involves deploying services, CronJobs, and so on, and handling certification for TLS communication between the end user and services. cert-manager makes the process smoother with predefined CRDs to create, regenerate, and issue certificates.
- Kubernetes is a good platform for applying deployment strategies such as `RollingUpdate`, `Blue-Green`, and canary. `RollingUpdate` is the default deployment strategy in which pods are gradually updated until they all have up-to-date resource descriptions. `Blue-Green` works as a switch, and canary is good for showcasing experimental features to end users for a specific time.

# Part 3

# gRPC and microservices architecture

There are three types of companies in software architecture: those that are content with their monolith applications, those that plan to switch to microservices, and those that already use microservices in production. Each company has its reasons for choosing a particular architecture, but using microservices comes with its own set of challenges. For instance, when you decide to break down a monolith application into services, you need to figure out how to manage communication between the services.

In part 1, we will first look at the big picture of an e-commerce application, and then delve into microservices architecture and its critical requirements, such as fault tolerance, security, continuous integration/continuous deployment (CI/CD), public access, and scaling, among others. Proper communication patterns between microservices are essential, and we will cover this topic as well.

We will also introduce gRPC and show how it fits into a microservices environment for service-to-service communication. You will become familiar with gRPC and see how it prioritizes security and performance to give you a seamless experience.

# *Observability*

**This chapter covers**

- Understanding observability concepts, such as traces, metrics, and logs
- Adding OpenTelemetry instrumentation libraries to ship metrics to a metrics collector
- Setting up a performance monitoring dashboard for microservices using Jaeger and Prometheus
- Installing an observability stack that includes Jaeger, Prometheus, Fluent Bit, Elasticsearch, and Kibana

Due to the nature of microservice architecture, you may end up with many services to meet product needs. Having good visibility of this system becomes important for being proactive about spotting problems and taking quick action to fix them. Services talk to other services, databases, queues, and third-party services, which produces insights about internal operations. In this chapter, we learn how to collect those insights and generate meaningful reports to understand situations in a cloud-native microservices environment.

> **About code examples in this chapter**
> In chapter 4, we started coding our services; in this chapter, we depend on what we implemented from chapters 4 through 8. The examples in this chapter are complete, and you can run the entire application by checking the README file in the repository. We will continue to extend the application to see how observability works.

## 9.1   *Observability*

Microservice architecture is a distributed system in which services communicate to maintain data consistency. Let's say that `PlaceOrder` visits three services to create an order, charge a customer's credit card, and ship it to the customer. An error can occur in any of those services while handling a `PlaceOrder` operation, and this is where the challenge begins. Observability helps us track a problem's root cause by analyzing traces, metrics, and logs. This chapter will show how observability can be perfectly handled in a microservices system that uses gRPC for communication. In this context, observability can answer the following questions:

- Why did the product service crash yesterday?
- Why is performance degraded in the middle of the day each Thursday?
- What is the performance of the Payment service like right now?

To answer these questions, we need a proper observability system that shows traces, metrics, and logs in the correct format so that we can analyze them and take action. We will use different technologies such as Jaeger (https://www.jaegertracing.io/), OpenTelemetry (https://opentelemetry.io/), and Prometheus (https://prometheus.io/), but first let's look at what traces, metrics, and logs are in a microservices environment.

### 9.1.1   *Traces*

A *trace, a collection of operations to handle a unique transaction,* refers to the journey of a request across services in a distributed system. It encodes the metadata of a specific request to propagate it until it reaches its final service. A trace can contain one or more spans that map to a single operation (see figure 9.1).

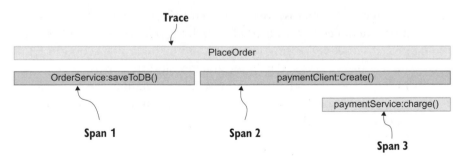

**Figure 9.1   Journey of a request**

As shown in figure 9.1, the name of the journey is `PlaceOrder`, and once it is initialized, a trace ID is automatically generated. Then it spans to multiple parts such as saving in the database and then calling the Payment service via the payment client. The payment client call process also creates another span while it is in the Payment service to make a query in a logging backend using a trace ID and sorting it by date in ascending order to see what happened to the request. We can see gRPC-related metadata in spans under a specific trace (figure 9.2).

Figure 9.2 is for a sever span that contains information about a single operation: the entry point of `payment.Create`. Keys are already implemented within the specific instrumentation library contracted by the OpenTelemetry project. (You can see all instrumentation libraries here https://opentelemetry.io/docs/instrumentation/.) `rpc` `.service` and `rpc.method` refer to the gRPC service name and gRPC method name under that service, respectively. `span.kind` is used for pointing out if instrumentation is done on either the client or server side. Finally, `rpc.system` shows what sort of RPC is used in service communication, in this case gRPC. Now that we understand how trace and span work together, let's look at what metrics we can have in a microservices environment.

| Span key | Span value |
|---|---|
| rpc.service | Payment |
| rpc.method | Create |
| span.kind | server |
| rpc.system | grpc |

**Figure 9.2    Span tags**

### 9.1.2    Metrics

Metrics contain numerical values to help us define a service's behavior over time. Prometheus has metrics that are defined by name, value, label, and timestamp. Using these fields, we can see metrics over time. We can also group them using their labels. Of course, we can apply other aggregation techniques (https://prometheus.io/docs/prometheus/latest/querying/functions/) using metric fields, SLA, SLO, and SLI, and obtain information about the system. For more in-depth information, see Google's Site Reliability Engineering book (https://sre.google/sre-book/table-of-contents/).

#### SLA

An SLA (service-level agreement) is an agreement between customers and service providers and contains measurable metrics such as latency, throughput, and uptime. It is not easy to measure and report SLAs, so a stable observability system is important.

#### SLI

An SLI (service-level indicator) is a specific metric that helps showcase service quality to customers by referencing request latency, error rate, and throughput for example. The statement "The throughput of our service is 1000/ms" indicates that this service can handle 1,000 operations per millisecond.

#### SLO

A SLO (service-level objective) is the goal for a product team to satisfy SLA. Especially in SaaS projects, you can see the SLA in terms and conditions pages. A typical example of a SLO is "99.999% uptime for the Object Storage service": the Object Storage service should be up 99.999%, and it might be down 0.001% of the time. These numbers are calculated as average values (figure 9.3).

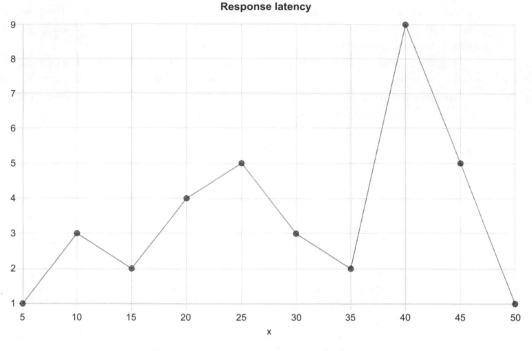

**Response latency**

**(1 + 3 + 2 + 4 + 5 + 3 + 2 + 9 + 5 + 1) / 10 = 4ms**

**Figure 9.3    Response latency over time**

As you can see in figure 9.3, the result is found by adding latency amounts (ms) and dividing them by the sampling count of 10. This is also called the *average value of numbers*. If I was using SLA documentation, I would say, "We provide a 4 ms response latency guarantee for our services." Can you spot the problem here? What if you have a 1,000 times 1 ms response latency and ten times 4 seconds latency?

$$10,00 \times 1 \text{ ms} + 10 \times 4,000 \text{ ms} = 5,000 \text{ ms}$$

$$5,000,\text{ms} / 1010 = 5,\text{ms}$$

Even though you had a very good response latency of 1 ms, the remaining ten response latencies corrupted your report. Averaging numbers may not satisfy customers; they might want to see the distribution of latencies with their percentages. There is a term to explain this situation: *percentile*. For example, if you say, "The 95th percentile response latency is 3 ms," 95% of the response latencies are 3 ms or less.

Think about the response latency numbers in figure 9.4.

| 10 | 22 | 2 | 3 | 9 | 1 | 87 | 11 | 7 | 4 |
|----|----|----|----|----|----|----|----|----|----|

**Figure 9.4  Response latencies**

The first thing we can do is sort all the numbers in descending order, which results in the numbers shown in figure 9.5.

| 87 | 22 | 11 | 10 | 9 | 7 | 4 | 3 | 2 | 1 |
|----|----|----|----|----|----|----|----|----|----|

**Figure 9.5  Order response latencies**

To find $80^{th}$ percentile response latency, see the index at 80% from the right to left direction, which in this case is 11 ms.

### 9.1.3 Logs

Applications produce events, and it is important to be aware of them to take action in case of an error or any kind of warning message. In this section, we will check the logging architecture first, then set up a logging system to ship gRPC microservices logs to the logging backend.

In monolithic applications, saving produced logs in a file to read later is not difficult. In microservices, you can still save logs in files, but combining different log files is challenging. Saving logs locally is not the only option; we can also ship them to a central location. In a Kubernetes environment, we have two types of logging architecture:

- Node-level logging
- Cluster-level logging

Let's look at both.

#### NODE-LEVEL LOGGING

In node-level logging architecture, applications generate events, which are logged to a file or standard output using some logging library in the application. If the application keeps logging events, that file can grow dramatically, which will make it hard to find certain logs. To avoid this situation, we can use log rotation: once a log file reaches a specific size, it can be rotated to a file with a name that contains time metadata for that rotation. Once you rotate logs, they are saved in separate files, but we still need to ship them to a central location or find a way to analyze them in multiple files (figure 9.6).

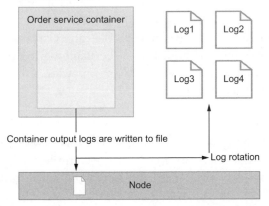

**Figure 9.6  Node-level logging architecture**

Some libraries can collect all the logs from containers and generate other artifacts.

### CLUSTER LEVEL LOGGING

There are agents, typically a daemonset, on each Kubernetes cluster node that are responsible for collecting logs from container-standard output logs. In cluster-level logging architecture, the logs are saved to a file on the host, but this time a central agent, (e.g., Elasticsearch, https://www.elastic.co/; graylog, https://www.graylog.org/) collects those logs and sends them to the logging backend. In figure 9.7, logging backends are not simply services that accept logging requests and serve them; they can also have components to show dashboards about logs and create alarms.

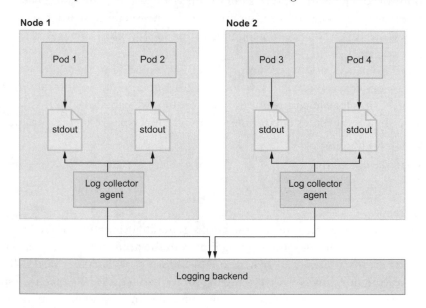

**Figure 9.7   Cluster-level logging architecture**

You have probably heard about the ELK stack, Elasticsearch-Logstash-Kibana: Elasticsearch is the logging backend, Logstash is some kind of log collector, and Kibana is the UI for logs, a proper monitoring dashboard for gRPC microservices that gives insight into services such as error rates and check details. We can even create alarms to send a notification to the development team if there is a matching log pattern in the logging backend store. Now that we understand tracing, metrics, and logs, let's look at how these work in the Kubernetes environment.

## 9.2    *OpenTelemetry*

OpenTelemetry (https://opentelemetry.io/) is a collection of SDKs and APIs that helps applications generate, collect, and export metrics, traces, and log information. OpenTelemetry is an umbrella project; you can see the implementation in different languages. We will use this project's Go version (https://opentelemetry.io/docs/instrumentation/go/). How can OpenTelemetry help us in a gRPC microservices project? Let's see the answer together.

### 9.2.1  Instrumentation locations

In a gRPC microservices project, services contact each other, so the client connection is a good candidate for generating insight into an application. When a client connects to the server, we can also generate observability data on the server side. We can even collect insights from database-related calls, and we already have an OpenTelemetry GORM extension (https://github.com/uptrace/opentelemetry-go-extra/tree/main/otelgorm) that helps us collect DB operations. With proper instrumentation setup, we can also allow OpenTelemetry plug-ins to propagate tracing information to the next services. Let's look at how to handle collection with minimum effort.

### 9.2.2  Instrumentation

In the gRPC world, it is very common to use interceptors to handle common things in a central place instead of implementing them manually by duplicating different packages. Instrumentation has gRPC support—a set of interceptors that collect gRPC metrics and make them available to send to metric collector backend such as Jaeger. Once we add these interceptors to client calls, the Order service calls the Payment service via the payment adapter, and all the requests to the Payment service are intercepted to collect data and make it available to ship to the metric backend:

```
...
var opts []grpc.DialOption
    opts = append(opts,
        grpc.WithTransportCredentials(insecure.NewCredentials()),
        grpc.WithUnaryInterceptor(otelgrpc.UnaryClientInterceptor()),   ◄──
    )
    conn, err := grpc.Dial(paymentServiceUrl, opts...)
...
```

**An interceptor for OpenTelemetry gRPC integration**

In chapter 5, we used gRPC interceptors to handle retry operations and create resilient systems. In this example, we use the same notation by adding an interceptor to a dial option so that the client connection will know how to collect and send telemetry data. In our case, telemetry data is generated while the Order service calls the Payment service.

The next step is to add those instrumentations to our codebase and first look at how we can prepare a metric backend, then provide the metrics' backend URL for instrumentation.

### 9.2.3  Metric backend

gRPC microservices generate metrics for different components, and those metrics become helpful if we process them to generate actionable reports. OpenTelemetry

SDKs help us instrument gRPC microservices quickly and require a metric collector endpoint to send them for future processing. We will use Jaeger, an open source distributed tracing system developed by Uber Technologies, to store our metrics and generate meaningful dashboards to understand what is happening in the microservices environment. Jaeger is good for handling metrics that come from OpenTelemetry; it uses a metric store such as Cassandra to complete a set of queries to show it in the Jaeger UI. Jaeger also allows us to save metrics in another store such as Prometheus to show microservices' performance in a monitoring dashboard.

Next, we will complete a step-by-step installation of observability tools to collect and visualize system insights. Let's look at the overall picture metrics' backend architecture; then we can continue with Kubernetes-related operations.

### 9.2.4    *Service performance monitoring*

In the service performance monitoring component of Jaeger (figure 9.8), applications send OpenTelemetry data to the Jaeger collector endpoint, and Jaeger also sends it to Prometheus to store it in a time series format. Since we have time series data, it is easy for Jaeger to generate response latency graphs based on time using Prometheus queries. This will show percentile metrics over time.

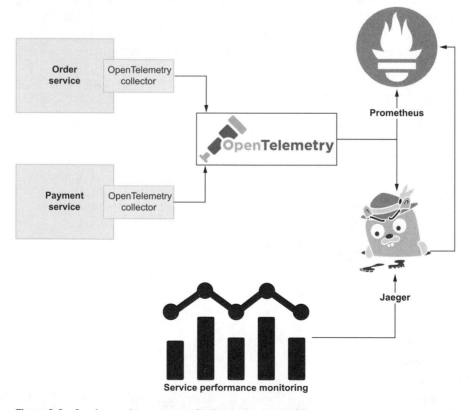

**Figure 9.8    Service performance monitoring in the Jaeger UI**

In the Jaeger UI, we also see a tracing query screen to find traces by service name and check request flow by their latencies. For example, we can see the latency distribution for each service after the client sends a `PlaceOrder` request. Now that we understand the initial picture of the metrics backend and what we can do with Jaeger components, let's go back to the Kubernetes environment and set up all those architectures for observability.

## 9.3 Observability in Kubernetes

As mentioned, we will use Jaeger and Prometheus for our metrics backend. To install them, we will use Helm Chart, a dependency management tool for the Kubernetes environment. Plenty of charts help install Jaeger, but because there is no option with both Prometheus and Jaeger, I implemented one (https://artifacthub.io/packages/helm/huseyinbabal/jaeger) that includes three components: Jaeger All in One, which has all Jaeger components; OpenTelemetry Collector for collector endpoint; and Prometheus. Let's look at what kind of information they expose.

### 9.3.1 Jaeger All in One

Jaeger All in One uses the `jaegertracing/all-in-one` (https://hub.docker.com/r/jaegertracing/all-in-one/) Docker image to serve Jaeger components. We will use Helm Chart to deploy this, which exposes the ports in figure 9.9 (http://mng.bz/KeGE).

| Port | Protocol | Component | Function |
|------|----------|-----------|----------|
| 6831 | UDP | agent | accept `jaeger.thrift` over Thrift-compact protocol (used by most SDKs) |
| 6832 | UDP | agent | accept `jaeger.thrift` over Thrift-binary protocol (used by Node.js SDK) |
| 5775 | UDP | agent | (deprecated) accept `zipkin.thrift` over compact Thrift protocol (used by legacy clients only) |
| 5778 | HTTP | agent | serve configs (sampling, etc.) |
| 16686 | HTTP | query | serve frontend |
| 4317 | HTTP | collector | accept OpenTelemetry Protocol (OTLP) over gRPC, if enabled |
| 4318 | HTTP | collector | accept OpenTelemetry Protocol (OTLP) over HTTP, if enabled |
| 14268 | HTTP | collector | accept `jaeger.thrift` directly from clients |
| 14250 | HTTP | collector | accept `model.proto` |
| 9411 | HTTP | collector | Zipkin compatible endpoint (optional) |

**Figure 9.9  General ports used in a Jaeger All in One deployment image**

These ports are primarily used in Jaeger-related operations, such as viewing metrics on the Jaeger UI. gRPC microservices will also send their traces to the OpenTelemetry Collector in the Helm Chart. Let's look at what the OpenTelemetry Collector exposes for gRPC microservices.

### 9.3.2 *OpenTelemetry Collector*

OpenTelemetry Collector uses `otel/opentelemetry-collector-contrib` (https://hub .docker.com/r/otel/opentelemetry-collector-contrib), which exposes two ports: `14278` and `8889`. `14278` is for the collector endpoint; it accepts metric requests from gRPC microservices. `8889` is used for the Prometheus exporter, and Jaeger uses this port to get time series data for performance monitoring. Once the collector obtains the values, it also sends calculated data to Prometheus.

### 9.3.3 *Prometheus*

We need Prometheus for Jaeger to store service insights in a time series format. The Helm Chart also provisions Prometheus, but you may want the existing Prometheus to be used in Jaeger All in One deployment. We can add the following environment variables to the Jaeger All in One deployment to enable the Prometheus metrics storage type:

```
METRICS_STORAGE_TYPE=prometheus
PROMETHEUS_SERVER_URL=http://jaeger-
➡ prometheus.jaeger.svc.cluster.local:9090
```

`jaeger-prometheus` is the Prometheus service name, `jaeger` is the namespace, and `svc.cluster.local` is the suffix used for Kubernetes service discovery. Now that we know all the components in the Helm Chart, let's deploy them to our local Kubernetes cluster.

### 9.3.4 *Jaeger installation*

We must add a repo for the Helm Chart with the following command:

```
helm repo add huseyinbabal https://huseyinbabal.github.io/charts
```

It will add my repo to your local Helm repositories list. Then we are ready to deploy Jaeger with all components:

```
helm install my-jaeger huseyinbabal/jaeger -n jaeger –create-namespace
```

This will install all the resources in the `jaeger` namespace, which will be created if it does not already exist. You can verify the installation by checking if Jaeger, OpenTelemetry, and Prometheus pods exist in your cluster.

Now that we have our metrics backend ready, we can continue changing our microservices to use OpenTelemetry SDKs to send data to the collector endpoint (http://jaeger-otel.jaeger.svc.cluster.local:14278/api/traces). Traces are sent to the OpenTelemetry Collector.

### 9.3.5 *OpenTelemetry interceptor for the Order service*

In this section, we will add the OpenTelemetry interceptor to the Order service, which will collect server-side metrics. Regardless of who calls the Order service, traces and metrics will be sent to the Jaeger OpenTelemetry Collector URL. To enable such a feature in the gRPC service, we will do two things:

- Configure the tracing provider.
- Add the OpenTelemetry interceptor to a gRPC service.

When you configure a tracing provider, you enable a global tracing configuration in your project, and that is the entry point of our services: `main.go`. This configuration includes adding an exporter, the Jaeger exporter in our case, and configuring the metadata so that tracing SDK can expose that metadata to the tracing collector. This collection operation is handled in batches, meaning the server-side metrics will be collected and sent in a batch instead of sending each metric individually. Here's the high-level implementation of this provider config:

```
import (
    "go.opentelemetry.io/otel"
    "go.opentelemetry.io/otel/attribute"
    "go.opentelemetry.io/otel/exporters/jaeger"
    "go.opentelemetry.io/otel/sdk/resource"
    tracesdk "go.opentelemetry.io/otel/sdk/trace"
    semconv "go.opentelemetry.io/otel/semconv/v1.10.0"    Configures the
)                                                         Jaeger exporter
...
func tracerProvider(url string) (*tracesdk.TracerProvider, error) {
    exp, err :=
     jaeger.New(jaeger.WithCollectorEndpoint(jaeger.WithEndpoint(url)))  ◁
    if err != nil {
        return nil, err
    }
    tp := tracesdk.NewTracerProvider(           Exports the tracing        The URL that contains
        tracesdk.WithBatcher(exp),      ◁       metrics in a batch        the OpenTelemetry
        tracesdk.WithResource(resource.NewWithAttributes(                 schema
            semconv.SchemaURL,                              ◁
            semconv.ServiceNameKey.String(service),   ◁
            attribute.String("environment", environment),   An attribute that
            attribute.Int64("ID", id),                       describes the
        )),                                                  service name
    )
    return tp, nil
}
```

An arbitrary ID that can be used in tracing the dashboard

This tracing configuration define service metadata that will be used globally. You can see metadata attributes such as service name, ID, and environment added to the tracing provider configuration. We can see those attributes in the Jaeger tracing UI and search by those attributes. SchemaURL also understands the schema contract of telemetry data.

To use this function in the Order Service, go to the order folder in the microservices project and add the function to the cmd/main.go file. You can automatically execute go mod tidy to fetch the newly added function dependencies. As you can see, this is only a function definition; to initialize the tracing provider, we can add it to the beginning of the main function:

```
func main() {
    tp, err := tracerProvider("http://jaeger-                    Tracing collector
    ➥ otel.jaeger.svc.cluster.local:14278/api/traces")    ◄─────┘ endpoint
    if err != nil {
        log.Fatal(err)
    }                                       Sets the tracing provider
                                            through the OpenTelemtry SDK
    otel.SetTracerProvider(tp)    ◄─────
    otel.SetTextMapPropagator(propagation.NewCompositeTextMapPropagator(pro
    ➥ pagation.TraceContext{}))    ◄──────
    ...                                    Configures the
}                                          propagation strategy
```

In the tracing provider configuration, we simply provide a tracing collect endpoint, which we installed via the Helm Chart, and set the tracing provider using OpenTelemetry SDK. Then we configure the propagation strategy to propagate traces and spans from one service to another. For example, since the Order service calls the Payment service to charge a customer, existing trace metadata will be propagated to the Payment service to see the whole request flow in the Jaeger tracing UI. Now that the Order service knows the tracing provider, let's add a tracing interceptor to the gRPC service.

OpenTelemetry has a registry system in which you can see various instrumentation libraries (https://opentelemetry.io/registry/). When you search for gRPC, you can find gRPC instrumentation that contains a gRPC interceptor. We can add our interceptor as an argument to the gRPC server in this file. Remember that we already have a gRPC server implementation in each service, which you can see in internal/adapters/grpc/server.go:

```
import (
"go.opentelemetry.io/contrib/instrumentation/google.golang.org/grpc/otelgrpc"
)
...
grpcServer := grpc.NewServer(
        grpc.UnaryInterceptor(otelgrpc.UnaryServerInterceptor()),
    )
...
```

Notice that interceptor comes from the otelgrpc package, which you can find in the OpenTelemetry instrumentation registry. Now, whenever we call the Order service, the server metrics will be sent to the Jaeger OpenTelemetry Collector endpoint and be accessible from the Jaeger UI. You can find the pod named `jaeger` and do a port forward for port `16686`, Jaeger's UI port. For example, if the pod name is `jaeger-c55bf4988-ghfsd`, the following command in the terminal will open a proxy for port `16686` to access the Jaeger UI:

```
kubectl port-forward jaeger-c55bf4988-ghfsd 16686
```

You can then access the Jaeger UI by visiting http://localhost:16686 in the browser, as shown in figure 9.10.

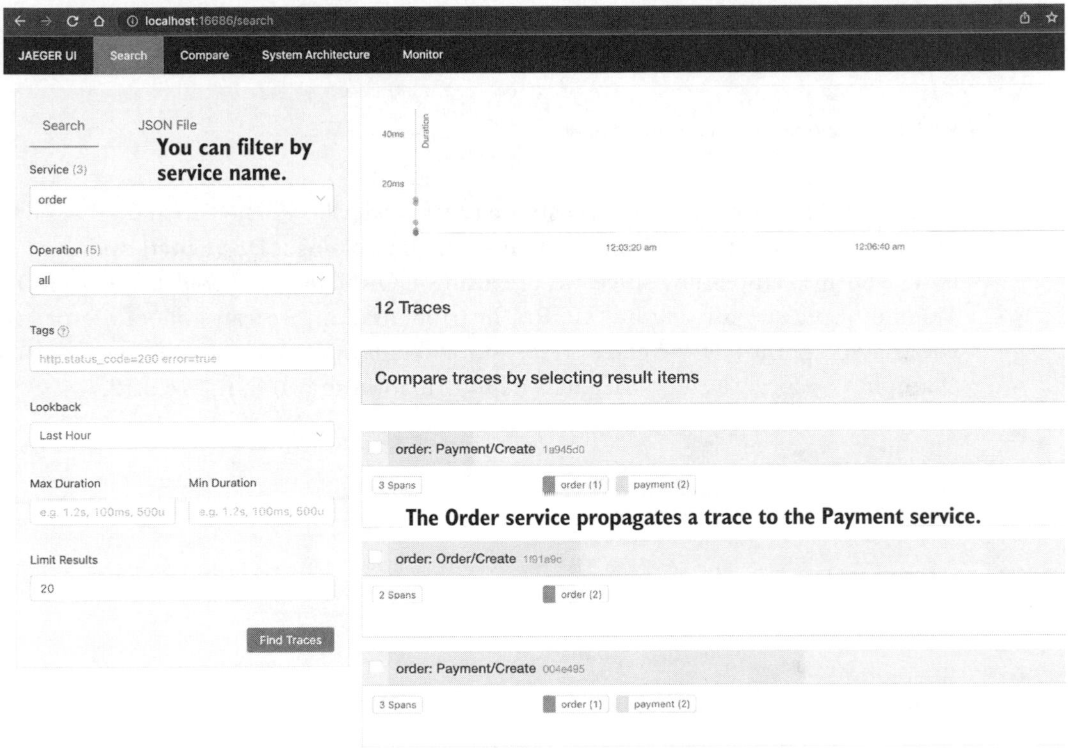

**Figure 9.10   Jaeger UI for tracing**

The tracing search screen is a simple interface that allows you to search for traces and see more details by clicking on the spans. In figure 9.11, you can see examples in which the Order service has one span and the Payment service two spans. Let's look at how we can use those details to understand service metrics.

### 9.3.6   *Understanding the metrics of the Order service*

The request generates traces and spans while it visits each service, and those spans contain useful metrics about services. With the tracing provider's help, we can ship those traces and metrics to collector endpoints in the Jaeger ecosystem. We already checked a very basic example in the previous section, and now we will review a specific trace to understand what is going on in it. From the Jaeger UI (figure 9.10), we will see the details in figure 9.11 after clicking the first trace.

**Figure 9.11   Span details of the create order flow**

In figure 9.11, it took 4.2 ms to finish the create order flow. The `Payment Create` operation in the Payment service took 3.36 ms, which contains a DB-related operation that took 2.88 ms. Hopefully, since we are using GORM in our project and the OpenTelemetry registry already has GORM instrumentation, we can collect metrics from DB-related operations. We can also see more details by clicking any of those spans. For example, `payment/PaymentCreate` has the information shown in figure 9.12.

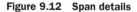

**Figure 9.12   Span details**

As you can see, there is plenty of metadata in span details, and `rpc.service` was defined in our tracing provider, as well as the ID and environment. (You can see the description of the fields in figure 9.12 here: http://mng.bz/9DY0.) `span.kind` was also defined, which shows us this is a server-related metric. Let's look at another example.

In a DB operation, you can see `database`, `statement`, and so on. These metrics are helpful to spot the root cause of a problem, as the provided SQL statement can provide a lot of information, such as the performance of the query. You can check traces, spans, and related metrics, as well as the performance summary of gRPC microservices using the Jaeger service performance monitoring (SPM) component (figure 9.13).

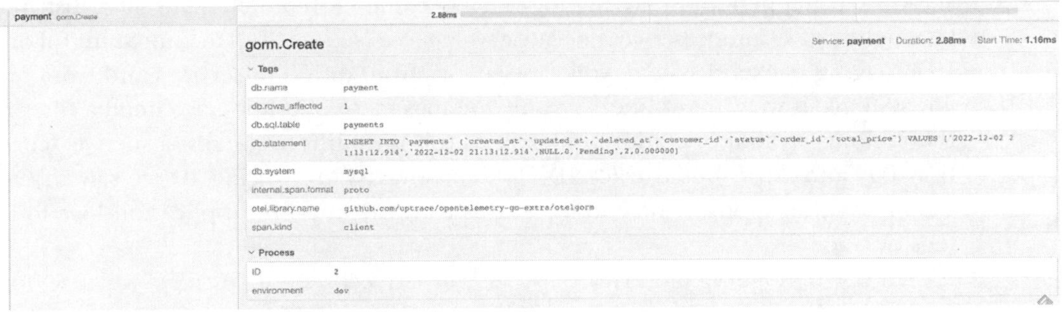

**Figure 9.13    DB-related span details**

### Jaeger SPM

In SPM, you can see the performance monitoring metrics for each service after clicking the Monitor menu in Jaeger UI. To understand the basic performance analysis of the Order service, select Order in the dropdown menu to see a performance summary that contains p95 latency, request rate, error rate, and so on (figure 9.14).

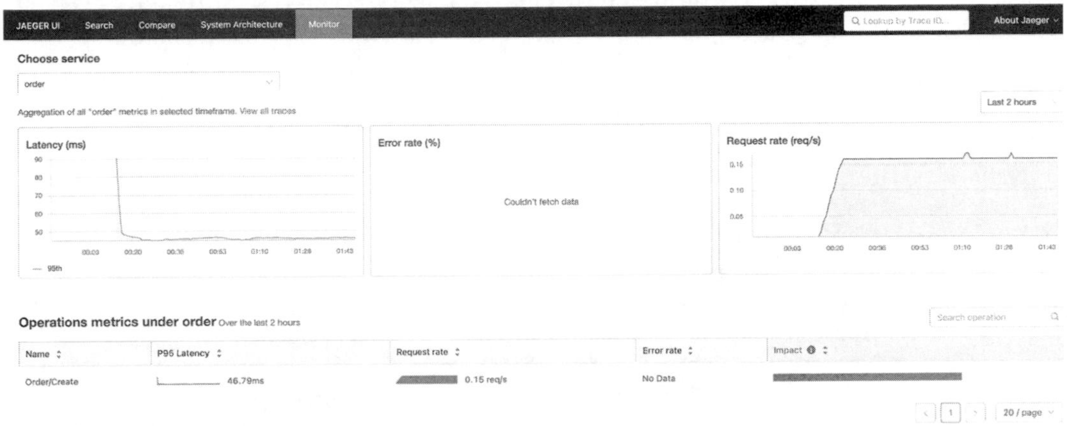

**Figure 9.14    Jaeger SPM**

In figure 9.14, the p95 latency of the Order service is 46.79 ms, meaning 95% of the latencies are 46.79 ms or less. You can also see the frequency of the requests: 6 per second. As a reminder, these performance metrics are aggregated from Prometheus. Now that we have checked traces and metrics, let's look at how we can handle logs in Kubernetes.

### 9.3.7  *Application logging*

Application logs are important to reference when we have a problem in the live environment because they contain messages from the application that can help us understand what happened. Analyzing logs may become more challenging in a distributed system like gRPC microservices because we need to see the logs in a meaningful order. In a logging backend system, you can see logs from different services and from different systems. If we want to filter for only the logs in an operation, we need a filter field that belongs to that operation. I have seen this with different names, such as "correlation ID" and "distributed trace ID," which refer to the tracing ID we saw in Open-Telemetry. Let's look at how to inject this trace ID into our application logs to filter logs by trace IDs.

Plenty of logging libraries exist in the Go ecosystem, but we will use logrus (https://github.com/sirupsen/logrus) in our examples. Here's a simple example:

```
log.WithFields(log.Fields{
    "id": "12212"
  }).Info("Order is updated")
```

After using this code, a message with metadata and key-value pairs is provided in standard output. In this example, order ID metadata is inside a log message, so if you ship this message to the logging backend, you can filter logs using that metadata.

Let's go back to distributed systems. To inject trace and span IDs into every log we printed using the logrus library, we can configure it to use a log formatter:

```
...
type serviceLogger struct {                              Logs will be printed
    formatter log.JSONFormatter    ◁──────               in JSON format.
}

                                                         Gets the
                                                         span from
func (l serviceLogger) Format(entry *log.Entry) ([]byte, error) {    the context
    span := trace.SpanFromContext(entry.Context)    ◁──────
    entry.Data["trace_id"] = span.SpanContext().TraceID().String()
    entry.Data["span_id"] = span.SpanContext().SpanID().String()
    //Below injection is Just to understand what Context has
    entry.Data["Context"] = span.SpanContext()
    return l.formatter.Format(entry)    ◁──────
}                                                  Injects the trace and span
...                                                into the current log message
```

This is just a definition of a log formatter, and when you look at the logic in the `Format` function, you can see it loads span data from context and configures the existing log entry to inject tracing data. How is this log formatter used? There are multiple answers to this question: you can pass this formatter to other packages to use it, or maybe put formatter initialization in the `init()` function to configure log formatting once the `main.go` is loaded:

```
func init() {                          ◁──── Executes the function on the file load
    log.SetFormatter(serviceLogger{
        formatter: log.JSONFormatter{FieldMap: log.FieldMap{   ◁─┐  Renames the
            "msg": "message",                                    │  log fields
        }},
    })
    log.SetOutput(os.Stdout)   ◁─┘
    log.SetLevel(log.InfoLevel)   ◁──── Sets the log level
}
```

Sets serviceLogger as the log formatter

Logs are printed in standard output.

Log formatters can be added to the cmd/main.go file, and once you add the `init()` function it, the log formatter will be initialized when the application starts. Then, you can use logrus in any location, and it will use that formatter globally in your project:

```
log.WithContext(ctx).Info("Creating order...")
```

If you make a gRPC call to `CreateOrder`, logrus will use the context to populate its content, which you can see in trace and span information:

```
{"Context":{"TraceID":"4a55375c835c1e0f78d5a0001b6f5f5d","SpanID":"1ab65b1c
982ee940","TraceFlags":"01","TraceState":"","Remote":false},"level":"in
fo","message":"Creatingorder...","span_id":"1ab65b1c982ee940","time":"2
022-12-04T06:37:25Z","trace_id":"4a55375c835c1e0f78d5a0001b6f5f5d"}
```

`TraceID` and `SpanID` fields can be used in the logging backend to filter and show the logs related to a specific operation. However, how can we get the `TraceID` to complete a filter operation? In gRPC, we use context to propagate tracing information between services, which can be injected into the response context so that we can use it.

As you can see in the example, the logs are in JSON format, and you may think this is hard to read in the standard output. However, this usage is very useful for logging backends because they can easily map JSON fields into search fields, which you can use while searching. If you use plain text logs, you need to develop a proper parser to help the logging agent or backend convert log messages into a more readable data structure. Now that we also understand how to inject tracing information into application logs, let's look at how we can collect logs from those applications.

### 9.3.8 Logs collection

You can get Kubernetes pod logs in the terminal with the following command:

```
kubectl logs -f order-74b6b997c-4rwb5
```

`kubectl` is not magic here, as whatever you write in the logs in standard output is stored in a log file in the file system. These log files have a naming convention, such as `<pod>_<namespace>_<container>-<unique_identifier>.log`, and are located in /var/log/containers in Kubernetes nodes. The post is that collecting logs is not that difficult; a simple agent could stream those files and process them. A typical log collection setup needs one log collection agent per Kubernetes node to reach the log files under /var/log/containers.

Figure 9.15 shows a log collector agent in every Kubernetes node that streams log files generated by the containers inside pods. These collector agents are mostly Kubernetes pods, and Kubernetes DaemonSets manage them to ensure there is one running process on each node, which allows you to access logs separately.

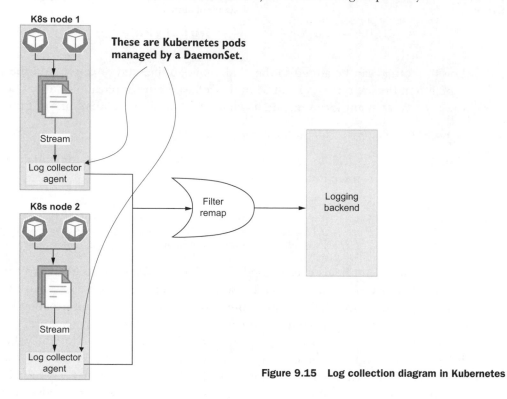

**Figure 9.15    Log collection diagram in Kubernetes**

We will use Fluent Bit (https://fluentbit.io/), an open source logs and metrics processor and shipper in a cloud-native environment, as a log collector agent. We can use Helm Charts to install Fluent Bit in the Kubernetes environment:

```
helm repo add fluent https://fluent.github.io/helm-charts
helm repo update
helm install fluent-bit fluent/fluent-bit
```

This will create a Kubernetes DaemonSet, which spins up a pod per Kubernetes node to collect logs. By default, it tries to connect Elasticsearch with the domain name elasticsearch-master, which means we must configure it via `values.yaml`. Before modifying `values.yaml`, let's look at how to use Elasticsearch and Kibana to make logs more accessible.

### 9.3.9    *Elasticsearch as a logging backend*

Elasticsearch is a powerful search engine based on Lucene (https://lucene.apache .org/core/). There are several options for using Elasticsearch, such as in AWS, GCP,

Azure Marketplace, or Elastic Cloud (https://www.elastic.co/). To better understand the logic, let's try to install Elasticsearch in our local Kubernetes cluster by installing CRDs dedicated to Elasticsearch components and installing the operator to create an Elasticsearch cluster:

```
kubectl create -f https://download.elastic.co/downloads/eck/2.5.0/crds.yaml
```

Since CRDs are available in Kubernetes, let's install the operator as follows.

```
kubectl apply -f https://download.elastic.co/downloads/eck/2.5.0/operator.yaml
```

Now that the CRDs and the operator are ready to handle the lifecycle of the Elasticsearch cluster, let's send an Elasticsearch cluster creation request:

```
cat <<EOF | kubectl apply -f -
apiVersion: elasticsearch.k8s.elastic.co/v1      ⟵── CRD spec for the cluster
kind: Elasticsearch
metadata:
  name: quickstart
spec:
  version: 8.5.2
  nodeSets:
  - name: default
    count: 1
    config:
      node.store.allow_mmap: false      ⟵── Disables memory mapping
EOF
```

To avoid disturbing the context, I will not dive deeply into an Elasticsearch-specific configuration, but you can read about virtual memory configuration (http://mng.bz/jPpV), which is used in this example. The previous command will apply the Elasticsearch spec to the Kubernetes cluster, which ends up deploying an Elasticsearch instance. Now we can configure Fluent Bit, but we need one more thing from Elasticsearch: a password. You can use the following command in your terminal to get a password:

```
PASSWORD=$(kubectl get secret quickstart-es-elastic-user -o go-
⟼ template='{{.data.elastic | base64decode}}')
```

This simply gets the secret value for `elastic` and decodes it so that you can reach it via `$PASSWORD` variable.

In Fluent Bit, we can focus on the config in `values.yaml`, especially the `outputs` section, which defines output destinations so that Fluent Bit can forward the logs to them. To achieve that, let's create a fluent.yaml file in the root of the microservices project and add the following config:

```
config:
  outputs: |
    [OUTPUT]
        Name es
        Match kube.*      ⟵── Forward log that matches kube
        Host quickstart-es-http      ⟵── Elasticsearch endpoint name
```

```
Default ┌──▶  HTTP_User elastic
  user  │     HTTP_Password $PASSWORD   ◁───── Authentication password
        │     tls On
        │     tls.verify Off      ◁───── Disables TLS verification
              Logstash_Format On
              Retry_Limit False
```

To provide more context for the config, the values we provided in the Host, HTTP_User, and HTTP_Passwd fields are all generated by Elasticsearch deployments. If you have an existing Elasticsearch cluster, you must provide your settings. By default, TLS is enabled for the client-elasticsearch connection, but since this is a local deployment, TLS verification is disabled. We also defined the log format as Logstash (https:// www.elastic.co/logstash/) and removed the limitation of the retry operation. If Fluent Bit fails on log forwarding to Elasticsearch, it will retry infinitely. As a final step, let's update the Fluent Bit Helm Chart:

```
helm upgrade --install fluent-bit fluent/fluent-bit -f fluent.yaml
```

Our application is running, the Elasticsearch logging backend is running, and Fluent Bit forwards logs to Elasticsearch. What about visualization? Let's look at how we can visualize our logs in the Kubernetes environment.

### 9.3.10 *Kibana as a logging dashboard*

Kibana (https://www.elastic.co/kibana/) is a data visualization dashboard for Elasticsearch. This UI application uses Elasticsearch as an API backend to aggregate a search dashboard. We installed CRDs in the previous section, which contain Kibana-related resources. To install Kibana in Kubernetes, you can apply a Kibana resource:

```
cat <<EOF | kubectl apply -f -
apiVersion: kibana.k8s.elastic.co/v1     ◁───── Specs for Kibana
kind: Kibana
metadata:
  name: quickstart
spec:
  version: 8.5.2
  count: 1
  elasticsearchRef:
    name: quickstart    ◁───── Reference to Elasticsearch backend
EOF
```

This will simply deploy Kibana, and you can access it via port forwarding to port 5601, the default port for Kibana. When you go to http://localhost:5601 in your browser, you may get a warning about defining the index. In that case, you can provide an arbitrary name and an index pattern (e.g., log*), which simply matches Logstash logs. Figure 9.16 shows the dashboard with Kubernetes logs.

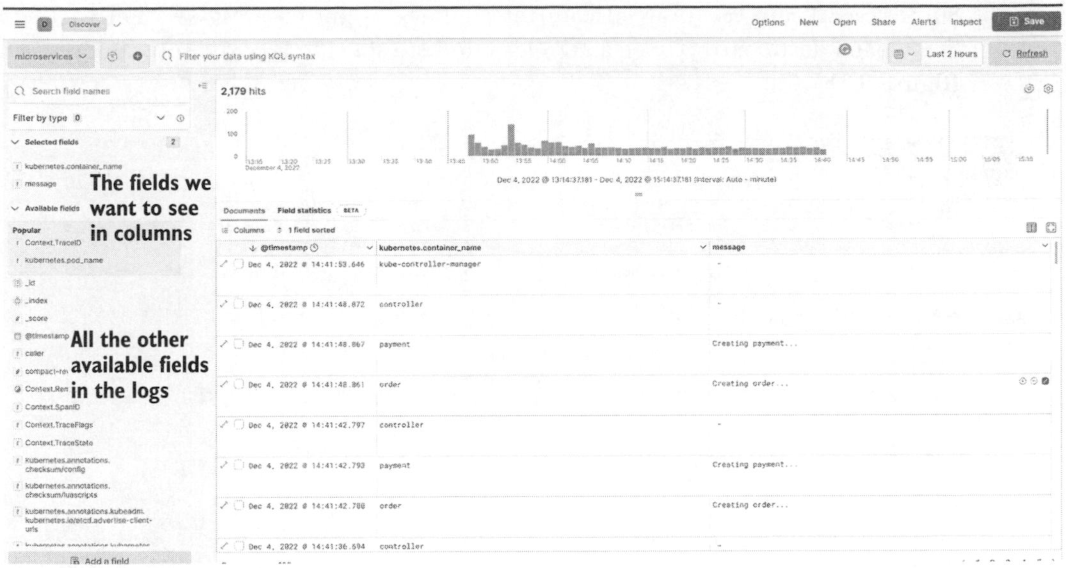

**Figure 9.16    Kibana logs dashboard**

As shown in figure 9.16, I selected only the `container name` and `message` fields. All the available fields are processed and shipped to Elasticsearch by Fluent Bit, which means you can modify the syntax in the Fluent Bit configuration based on your needs. If you click any logs there, you can see more details, as shown in figure 9.17.

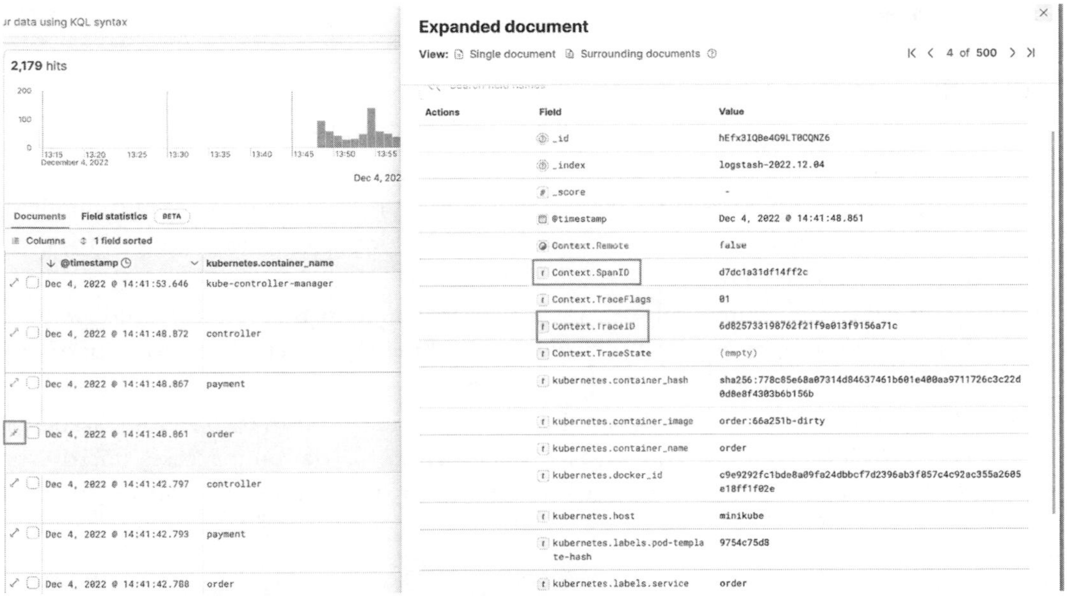

**Figure 9.17    Logs details that contain `TraceID` and `SpanID`**

Since `TraceID` and `SpanID` are already injected into application logs, we can see them in the Kibana dashboard. To see all the logs under a specific `TraceID`, you can do a search (figure 9.18).

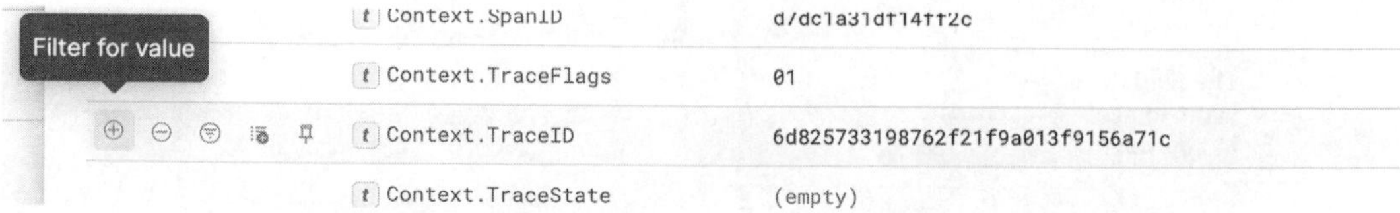

**Figure 9.18    Filter by `TraceID`**

You can see that the entire flow belongs to a specific `TraceID` (figure 9.19).

**Figure 9.19    Results grouped by `TraceID`**

## *Summary*

- Observability is key to successful, stress-free, and more visible microservices.
- The main components for observability are traces, metrics, and logs, and correlating them is important, as it allows you to detect why an application is slow, what the metrics are, and what the related logs are at the time a metrics anomaly is detected.
- Traces are important for understanding request flows in a microservices environment, especially if they have related metrics instrumented by OpenTelemetry SDKs.
- A cluster-level logging architecture with Fluent Bit as a collector, Elasticsearch as a logging backend, and Kibana as data visualization increases microservices' observability. This setup provides flexibility for searching structured log data.

# *index*